Rez Dogs Eat Beans

And Other Tales

by

Gordon Johnson

ISBN: 0-7596-6443-9

This book is printed on acid free paper.

1stBooks - rev. 11/08/01

Acknowledgements:

No man is an island. And this collection of columns needed help. First, thanks to Ruth Anderson Wilson who spearheaded this project. The book was her idea. It was her initiative and time that made it real. Supercharged, she jolted me with a cattle prod to make deadlines. Her counsel was invaluable.

Ruth assembled a committee: LaVaughn (Bonnie) Bussee, Marilyn Gallagher, Wilma Austin, Betty Rose, Mark Wilson and Paul Wilson who dutifully read almost 400 columns and sifted them down to 80 for this collection. I am in their debt.

Jill Richardson was the technical advisor without whom the book would never have happened. Her time spent on the project is most appreciated.

The cover art and assorted illustrations are by Robert Freeman, a consummate Indian artist and buddy from the Rincon Indian Reservation.

Another buddy, a *Press-Enterprise* photographer. Thomas Kelsey took on the tough job making me look good for the cover picture.

Finally, my thanks to Marcia McQuern, publisher of the *Press-Enterprise* for allowing these columns to be reprinted.

Acknowledgement is made to The Press-Enterprise of Riverside California, in which these columns first appeared

To obtain copies of this book contact: Ruth Anderson Wilson, PO Box 33024, Riverside, California 92519

Rez Dogs Eat Beans

Once my cousin Goose, who used to sport rich women in Palm Springs, brought an Afghan hound home to the Pala Indian Reservation.

My guess is that the dog was owned by some tanned, tennis-playing woman who decided to spend the summer sunning her wares on the French Riviera, and Goose couldn't abide just letting the dog mope in a kennel.

So he took pity on the thing. Pampered all his life, O.D. came high-stepping onto the reservation, silky hair brushed to a sheen, toenails clipped, teeth pearly white. A city dog.

O.D. was none too bright, either. Tell him to fetch, and he'd sit there looking goofy, as if saying, "Which way did they go, George? Which way did they, go?"

He ran like a 13-year-old boy who grew too fast. I can picture him now, all loose and gangly, padding down the dirt road toward Goose's house, singing, "I'm bringing home a baby bumble bee, won't my momma be so proud of me."

People used to make fun of O.D., myself included. It was plain he wasn't cut out for reservation hardships.

A couple of months later, you wouldn't have recognized poor O.D. Mud and twigs clung to his matted coat. He took to sleeping on the roof of Goose's car at night to make it harder for the other dogs to get at him. He seemed to have developed a nervous tic.

Needless to say, O.D. didn't last long on the rez. I'd like to think he's still loping across the desert, hellbound for his Palm Springs groomer. But more likely, he was hit by a gravel truck, or killed in a dog fight, or shot dead for chasing cattle.

Anyway, one day, he just disappeared.

Such is the fate of many reservation dogs, especially those not born to the life.

Nearly every reservation household has at least one dog. Many have two or three. With no fences, the dogs have the run of the place, free to do as they please.

In the morning, some chase rabbits through the willows and cottonwoods across the river. As the day heats up, they'll nap in the shade of the Mission San Antonio porch, or under the pepper tree behind the Pala Store.

Some dogs follow their kids to the mission school, where nuns throw blackboard erasers at them to chase them out of classrooms.

Others stick close to the back porch, ever watchful for a half-eaten tortilla roll tossed their way or a greasy frying pan that needs licking.

I get a kick out of dog food commercials, like the one where the guy's champion Weimaraners point quail and dive headlong into the pond to retrieve downed ducks.

With nutrients scientifically balanced, his dogs only eat the best, he boasts.

Reservation dogs eat beans. A dog that won't eat beans doesn't survive.

A woman who gossips too long at her friend's house and returns home to find her pot of beans scorched, doesn't throw them out. She dumps them into the dog dish.

"That ought to hold you for a few days," she says. Eat or starve. That's the rule.

Reservation dogs are tough. They're known for it.

People will say when trying to saw through a fried round steak: "This meat's tougher than a reservation dog."

Or: "That Rosie sure is cranky, she's meaner than a reservation dog."

Or: "Joe's chasing that skirt like he's a reservation dog."

Dogs born on the rez have the playful puppy days to form alliances. They find a place in the pecking order, and hold to it, or suffer a whipping.

A top dog will usually have one or two sidekicks he's groomed over the years to back his play.

There was once a burly dog, mottled black and blue, named Shindig, who ruled the reservation for what must have been a decade. Shindig was pure mutt, but like I said, a brute. His backup was a dog named Duke, a German shepherd skinny as a razor blade with teeth just as sharp.

They liked nothing better than to rain misery on unsuspecting newcomers.

Shindig would launch the frontal attack, while Duke went around back for the huevos. More than one reservation dog went around with a half-empty sack.

So it went. And so it goes. A dog's life on the rez.

Aunt Clara Still Laughing After All These Years

At first light, with the roosters still crowing, you'd find Aunt Clara Chutnicut bent over a grubbing hoe, whacking down the foxtails and mustard greens that choked her yard.

She was in her 70s then.

Looking back, I should have helped. But somehow, it seemed a natural part of spring to see her in her knitted cap and three sweaters, working around her old house. And too, I'm a lazy son of a gun.

But not her. Every morning for weeks, I'd be lifted from sleep by the steady metallic scrape of hoe against earth. Each swipe chided: "Get up you layabout, get up." Hell of an alarm clock, that early morning dose of guilt.

Her house, just down from my grandmother's, was a Pala Indian Reservation original, one of the two-room wooden houses shipped around the Horn and slapped together for the Cupeno Indians removed in 1903 from their ancestral homes in Warner Springs.

Buffeted by too many winter winds, her home listed badly to the east. Never painted, it had that gray, weathered sheen, and the windows were glazed over, like eyes clouded by glaucoma.

No, it wasn't much, but it was the home where she had rocked her baby, Johnny, to sleep when he had the colic. It was the home where the kitchen smelled of pork chops frying in a cast-iron skillet. It was the home where the dog lapped water from a bucket beneath the dripping faucet out back.

So each spring, Aunt Clara cleaned her yard in time for the mission's Corpus Christi procession in June. Lord knows she didn't want her yard to draw unpious glances from the Pala Mission priests. Hers would be no house of shame.

But that was more than 20 years ago. The old house is gone now, and Aunt Clara has since put down her hoe.

Born Aug. 14, 1902, age has caught up to her. And she had a stroke a few years ago that took its toll.

But neither age, nor failing health has broken her spirit, or stolen her laughter.

That's what I love most about Aunt Clara. Her laughter. When she laughs, her eyes light up behind her thick glasses, and everything becomes a kind of crazy joke. She has the laugh of a celebrant. A laugh that puts life in its place.

She has always delighted in the small pleasures. Before her stroke, she'd drink a cold beer when it was offered. She'd get giddy at dances, and twirl with the best of them. She'd eat with abandon. No fad diets for her. Even today, if you stopped for a visit, her sweater pockets might be stuffed with cookies. Sweets for the sweet.

Oh, she has an ornery side too. A diehard Dodgers fan, she defends them with passion. I once teased her about her slumping Dodgers. I didn't do it twice. She looked at me like I was weed and all she wanted was her hoe. Don't mess with the Dodgers.

And if you're smart, you won't bad-mouth Perry Mason in her presence, either. She worships him.

Before the days of color TV and cable, she would train her rabbit-ears on the only station that would halfway come in - Channel 6. Luckily, it was well stocked with

Perry Mason reruns, and she watched them religiously. Still does.

In her youth, she did some hobnobbing with celebrities.

After completing St. Boniface boarding school in Banning and a stint at St. Mary's College in Los Angeles, Aunt Clara went to work as a domestic for actress Loretta Young, where she met John Wayne, Randolph Scott, Clara Bow and many others. To this day, she keeps their yellowed photographs in a special box, treasures of her glory days.

She returned to Pala for good in about 1932.

On a table, next to her TV, there's a pink clock radio that looks like the first clock radio ever made.

For some 50 years, that clock has been ticking off the minutes of her life. A hard life, but a good life. An Indian life.

This weekend, Aunt Clara will be honored at Pala's Cupa Days fiesta as the oldest Cupeno Indian on the face of the earth.

I too will offer my regards. For she's one of the good ones. A gentle, but strong woman, who taught me when all else fails, laughter makes sense.

THE SQUIRREL BOYS

A foot trail still cuts through the gourd plants and tumbleweeds that now overrun the place, leading to what's left of the old house, where Robert Ardillo and his older brother, William, lived and died on the Pala Indian Reservation in Northern San Diego County.

Even on its best day, the house wasn't much. Maybe 10 feet wide by 25 feet long, built of thin wooden slats with a shingle roof, just big enough to hold a bed, a wood stove and a small table.

Several years ago, a wind-blown elderberry tree crashed through the roof, leaving only the windowless east wall standing. One good blow, and it too will topple.

Leftovers of the Ardillos' lives litter the yard. The galvanized tub where they washed. The chopping block where they split stove wood. The five-gallon bucket they carried water in.

But the Ardillos' legacy isn't measured in material goods. No,by most standards, they failed miserably in life. They didn't accumulate. They didn't procreate.

But there are other reasons to remember Robert and William Ardillo.

They were known as the Squirrel Boys.

Robert was born in 1897.

William was born a few years earlier in 1893. They were descended from the Kengish clan, which means squirrel in the Luiseno Indian language. The Kengish name was later translated by missionaries into the Spanish - Ardillo. And that's how they came to be called the Squirrel Boys.

And some thought them quite squirrely.

A curious pair, the brothers were hermits. They lived their entire lives in that same weather-beaten house, with no electricity or running water or company.

Although neither got on with people much, William was by far the more reclusive.

"If he saw you coming down the road, he would hide behind a tree until you passed," said Wayne Nelson, a buddy of mine from the La Jolla Indian Reservation.

About 6-foot-1, Robert was about four inches taller than William.

Once or twice a week, he'd walk to the Pala Store to fill the kerosene can for their lamps. While there, he might pick up some slab bacon and coffee, but only the essentials.

Sam Powvall of the nearby Pauma Indian Reservation used to talk Indian with Robert at the store. Although Robert spoke English, he was more comfortable with Indian, Powvall said.

To eat, they farmed. They always had a vegetable garden. And back in the days when they had a horse to plow with, they grew hay in the sandy bottom lands of the San Luis Rey River and sold it to area ranchers.

But when their horse died of old age, they gave up the hay business, and took to planting watermelons instead.

Every year, they cleared their eight acres. It could be 100 degrees in the midday, so hot even the flies hid in the shade, but they'd be out there bent over their hoes, whacking out weeds.

"They were tough old guys, real chiefs," said Dennis Subish, a man who knew them well when he was a kid.

"Worked all the time, never drank much or smoked, never bothered anyone. They were great old men."

But in the winter of 1969, William got pneumonia. Despite his protests, they made him go to the hospital in Escondido. He stayed for a week, but couldn't stand being cooped up, and simply walked out, still in his hospital gown. Not familiar with town, he didn't know what to do. He spent the night huddled in a doorway, until they found him nearly frozen the next morning.

But he wouldn't stay in the hospital, so they let him go home, where he died shortly thereafter.

A few days later, Subish ran into Robert out on the trail. Robert was dragging something heavy. It was a sack of coins, their life savings, and he was taking it to the store to cash it in.

Subish gave him a ride.

"He used that money to pay for his brother's funeral," Subish said.

With his brother gone, Robert hoed alone, and boiled coffee for one, staying by himself in the house where the wind whipped through the cracks and the rain seeped through the rotting shingle roof.

In 1982, I helped dig his grave beside the Pala Mission. And as I shoveled dirt for his final resting place, I couldn't help but admire this man who was content with so little.

Just Trying To Get a Line On A Real Lady

In the mid-1930s, she played on the Pala Indian Reservation in a faded print dress and Lil' Abner-style shoes.

She was a dark, diminutive Indian girl with straight black hair and a white-toothed smile, who lived with her grandmother, Esperanza Fidelio, in a ramshackle house in the middle of the village.

With found lumber, they built her an add-on on the side of the house with just enough square footage for a bed and a makeshift dresser. The dresser didn't need to hold much, she only had three dresses.

The winter wind seemed to whip right through the drafty add-on, Barbara said, "And my feet were always cold."

"When I grow up, I'll never have cold feet again," she would vow, trying to rub her feet warm beneath the thin blankets of her bed.

"Some nights, my grandmother would call me to come rub her stomach. She had stomach cancer, or as the Indians called it, latitho, and her stomach often hurt her," Barbara said.

With her small hands she would massage her grandmother's ailing abdomen, "and you could hear it grumbling," she said.

"Oh, that feels better," her grandmother would say, and they would drift off to sleep, "and it was so nice and warm in her bed," Barbara said.

The grandmother had stomach cancer for years, but didn't complain. Despite her illness, she did her best to keep her household going, and she did it with a joke on her lips and kindness in her heart.

There was no welfare in those days, and people had to work for their keep. They raised livestock, grew vegetables and worked on nearby ranches and farms to get by.

"My grandmother also made baskets, and I would go with her across the river to pick the grasses she used," Barbara said.

The baskets were sold to buy necessities.

Into this hard-scrabble life drove a woman in a black sedan. She wore shiny, silk dresses and velvet hats. Her hair was fashionably bobbed and waved, and she wore jewelry that sparkled in the light.

From the trunk of her car, she hauled out boxes of second-hand clothes and groceries like beans, flour and canned fruit. But best of all, she brought sweet breads and candies, rare treats for a reservation girl.

Her name was Mrs. Cook, and she was from Elsinore. She'd come on Saturday afternoons with her CARE packages, give candies to the kids, then sit and drink coffee with Esperanza.

On one trip, she asked Esperanza if it would be OK for Barbara to come stay with her for a week.

Esperanza consented, and Barbara sat in the passenger seat of the car, staring wide-eyed out the windows at passing new vistas.

Mrs. Cook's white, wood-slat house sat by its lonesome atop a knoll.

The house seemed huge and intimidating, compared to the reservation shacks she was used to.

"There was this great sun porch with windows all around it. On a table was a bowl full of grapefruit-sized glass balls tinted blue, pink and green. When the sun hit just right, they would light up like the aurora borealis," Barbara said. "I'd never seen anything like that before, and I'd sit there and look at them for hours, they were so beautiful."

Mrs. Cook lived in her house all by herself. Her main source of entertainment seemed to be the upright piano in the parlor. After dinner, she'd play for Barbara until it was time for bed.

"She was very nice to me, and I remember it as a wonderful time," Barbara said.

After a week, Mrs. Cook dutifully took Barbara home. And Barbara never went back.

"I guess I felt like Shirley Temple being taken in by this rich woman. It was a fantasy come true," Barbara said.

Barbara, who is my mother, sometimes wonders whatever happened to Mrs. Cook.

"I didn't even know her first name, because back then, children didn't address adults by their first names," my mom said.

But she must have been about 50 in the mid-1930s, lived by herself, and was a real lady, my mom said.

"I'd sure like to know more about her."

Anybody got any ideas about who Mrs. Cook was and whatever happened to her?

Reality Testing

A few weeks back, I wrote about a mystery woman named Mrs. Cook who once invited my mother to stay with her for a week.

It was the first real time away from home for my mother, Barbara **Johnson,** who was only 8 years old at the time, and the trip left lasting impressions on the young girl fresh from the Pala Indian Reservation.

To this day, my mother gets wistful when she describes the basket full of tinted glass balls Mrs. Cook kept on a table in her sun porch.

The orbs captivated my mother, the way they collected and reflected the light, so colorful and dazzling, so far removed from her life of beans three times a day back on the reservation.

Through her awe-struck eyes, my mother remembered Mrs. Cook as an uptown kind of woman who wore stylish silk dresses, sported expensive jewelry, and bobbed and permed her hair just like the elegant women in the fashion magazines did in the mid-1930s.

And my mother recalled the beautiful after-dinner music, when Mrs. Cook would sit in the parlor and let her fingers dance over the ivories.

To my mother, Mrs. Cook lived in a Shirley Temple world of linen napkins and polished silverware. And my mother has carried around the memories of that wondrous brief stay for more than half a century.

When Mrs. Cook dropped my mother back at home, she was never seen again. Every now and then, like when she sees a glass ornament at a rummage sale or when she sees an old movie on TV, my mother wonders what happened to the nice white woman who gave her a glimpse into the other side of life.

Several days after talking to my mother, I asked my grandmother what she remembered of Mrs. Cook. As it turns out, my Aunt Martha Chutnicut, my grandmother's sister, worked for Mrs. Gay Cook before my mother went for her stay there.

My Aunt Martha was only about 15 at the time, and had just gotten out of St. Boniface, the Indian boarding school up in Banning, when Mrs. Cook asked if she'd like to be a housekeeper.

Not altogether keen on the idea, my aunt agreed to be Mrs. Cook's housekeeper as long as she could go to high school while she was up there.

"Why, of course you can go to school," Mrs. Cook said.

So my aunt packed her few belongings and took the road trip to Corona (not Lake Elsinore as my mother thought).

When she got to the white house with the big sun porch, my aunt found that Mrs. Cook was married to an Army captain attached to March air field.

My aunt says her life at the Cooks quickly became one of hard work: cleaning house, cooking meals and washing clothes.

All was not right in the big white house on the grassy knoll.

Although not a big man, the Captain was an ornery man, and mean to his wife, my aunt said.

He was a boozer and he would come home loud and abusive after a night of drinking, and she was afraid of him, my aunt said. "It's odd to think of them like that because they were so high up," she said.

"I remember one night when Mrs. Cook said to me, `You better sleep with me tonight,' and we pushed dressers and tables in front of the bedroom door so he couldn't come in," she said.

"I only lasted a year at that house," my aunt said. "I worked so hard, and for very little money, and I couldn't go to school because there was so much work. And besides, I needed to come home and take care of my mother."

Shortly after she left, my aunt heard through the grapevine that something snapped in the Captain's head and he died.

And then Mrs. Cook got paralyzed.

"How did she get paralyzed?" I asked her.

"I don't know," my aunt said with a hint of malice in her voice. "All I know is that he was a very mean man."

"Later, I heard she died, too," my aunt said. "Too bad, she was awfully nice to the Indians. Couldn't play the piano worth a lick though."

And another dazzling glass ball falls onto the concrete porch step, shattering into a thousand shards of disillusionment.

When Fool Dogs Try To Dance With Big Cats

The other day, while cleaning up around my old lot, I spotted the small dirt mound where I buried one of the great dogs of my life.

As I stood by his weedy grave, I flashed back 18 years to the day I got him.

In the pound's chain-link kennels, dogs of all shapes and sizes yapped, spun circles and leaped against the wire mesh for attention.

But in one kennel, a floppy-eared boxer sat motionless, his head cocked to the side, his eyes locked on mine.

The card clipped to his kennel gate read: "Butch, an 8-month-old boxer. Needs fenced yard."

An incorrigible runaway, I figured. He had a fawn-colored coat with a white chest and matching socks. Even though his stub of a tail wagged while he sat, he was too proud to fawn over me.

This dog has personality, I thought to myself.

I took him home.

I had a 1965 Volkswagen Baja Bug at the time, with a back seat that folded down into a nice flat space for him to stay. But he wouldn't have it. He insisted on the passenger seat, riding with his head held high like a tuxedoed duke on his way to meet the duchess.

Fifteen minutes after I let Butch into the front yard of my grandmother's place, a full-grown Lab from down the road approached stiff-legged, growling low in his throat, black hair bristling along the back of his neck.

Strange dogs don't exactly get the welcome mat on the Pala Indian Reservation where I live.

Only 8-months-old, I figured Butch would cower a little, let the Lab sniff him over, and then back down from trouble.

But Butch stood his ground, arching his muscular neck, growling in return. The older Lab, angered by Butch's refusal to kowtow, bumped him. Butch flew into that dog like a rooster into a cock fight.

"Holy Toledo," I said, jumping in to break up the fight. "This dog is nuts."

It was the first of many fights I would have to break up, but despite his pugilistic bent, Butch had an endearing side.

My first daughter, Tyra, was born shortly after Butch arrived, and he quickly assumed the role of friend and protector.

When my wife pushed Tyra to the store in her stroller, Butch would always lead the way, practically daring other dogs to bother them.

None did.

To my surprise, my wife, never the world's biggest dog lover, allowed Butch to live inside with us when we moved to a little apartment in Pauma Valley.

Butch would watch over Tyra as she crawled around the living-room floor. She could clamber on his back, tug on his ears or whack him with a baby rattle, and he'd stoically let her have her way.

Back then, I was taking classes at the University of California at San Diego, and would come home after a late night of researching term papers in the library to find my wife and child cuddled on the bed with Butch curled below them, snoring like a lumberjack.

When Tyra was cutting her baby teeth, and fussing at 4 in the morning, I'd bundle her up in a baby backpack and take her for long moonlight walks down a brushy trail toward the San Luis Rey River to calm her. Of course, Butch wouldn't be left behind.

On one such walk, Butch flushed a skunk out of the thick willows. Thinking the skunk was a threat to us, he attacked. For 10 minutes Butch and the skunk fought a life-or-death battle. I don't know which was worse, the stink or the ruckus.

Butch eventually killed the skunk, but it took several tomato juice baths and a bottle of Old Spice before I could stand being around him again.

Once, while trapping in the back country with a friend, Butch happened upon a bobcat in a trap. Like a fool, he jumped into the middle of that cat, and quickly learned that a big cat was nothing to mess with. In short order, the cat split one ear down the middle, and covered his head with claw marks.

"What the heck was that?" Butch seemed to ask when he finally disentangled himself.

Yes, Butch was crazy, but for the five years I had him, I loved him. And it was a sad day when I found him one morning dead in his sleep.

Gone without a goodbye or a whimper.

Home In Time For Tamales And The Hop

When I was 7, sleep was hard to come by in the back of our 1954 Plymouth station wagon during the long haul down Highway 101 to my grandmother's house for Christmas.

Up in the front seat, mom and dad talked in hushed voices, their faces awash in eerie green from the dashboard lights.

In the back, headlights from the cars behind us splashed through the tailgate window, and to keep **busy,** I made pictures out of the shadowy designs flickering on the station wagon's headliner.

Bing Crosby crooned Christmas carols through the tinny speakers of our push-button AM radio, barely audible above the engine drone, and the low-pitched whine of rubber tires rolling over tarmac.

Mile after mile, I tossed and turned beneath the quilt that covered us kids, squeezing my eyes tight, hoping sleep would overtake me so I could get to my grandmother's house that much faster.

But excitement ruled out sleep. Instead of dreamland, I counted sheep to my baby brother's snores as he slept open-mouthed next to my ear.

I felt better when we pulled into Riverside, because I knew we were getting close. I sat up to get a better look at the Christmas garlands wrapped around downtown street lights and the twinkling "Merry Christmas" banners strung across stoplights on the main drag.

In those days, you could tell a good city by the quality of its Christmas displays. Santa Barbara was my favorite, but Riverside was a contender.

The 60 or so miles from Riverside to the Pala Indian Reservation seemed endless, but finally, my dad shut off the station wagon engine in front of my grandmother's adobe house.

The night air, lush with the scent of eucalyptus trees and fireplace smoke, smelled like home.

My grandfather, in blue jeans and a flannel shirt, opened the front door and yelled out from the porch, "Hepa, hepa, come on in, get out of the cold."

I ran to him with a hug. "Good to see you, boy," he said, smiling.

Next my grandmother came out from the kitchen, wiping her hands on a dish towel. "Oh, I prayed you guys would make it down safe," she cried, and she doled out hugs all around too.

With the door closed behind us, my grandfather stoked the flames in the brick fireplace with another oak log or two, until the room was bright with its blaze.

In my grandmother's kitchen, big pots steamed on the stove, and corn husks covered the counter tops where she made Christmas tamales by the dozens.

As a welcome-home snack, she spooned her red chili meat into fresh homemade flour tortillas, and passed them out. Talk about good.

After eating, we ran around the house, sliding in our socks on the linoleum floors, laughing and playing, until we could hardly keep our eyes open.

Gordon Johnson

I slept in my Uncle Copy's room, where the plaster walls were covered with pictures of ballplayers and boxers scissored from sports magazines.

The next morning, several reservation men came by in a stake-bed truck loaded with Christmas trees they had cut from Morgan Hill, land the Pala tribe owns up toward Palomar Mountain.

In trade for the tree, my grandfather gave the men a six pack of Lucky Lager and they stood out front for awhile, drinking and joking before moving on to the next house.

My teen-aged Aunt LeeAnn took charge of tree decorating, heaping on tinsel and ornaments until the branches drooped under the weight.

She sang Elvis Presley songs and danced The Hop as she worked.

That night, I buffed my one pair of dress shoes with an old sock, and put on a clean shirt for Midnight Mass at the Pala Mission.

The choir sang "Silent Night," and I could hear my Aunt Vivian's contralto voice rise above the rest. I fell asleep in the church pew with a good feeling that I was with family and friends.

Christmas morning, we opened presents, ate a big breakfast, and had a great time, except for the part when my grandfather came home full of wine and song and fell into the Christmas tree.

But even that I remember with fondness, that Christmas of 1958

Here's To Your Health, Grandmother

Remember, Grandmother, how in the cool mornings following a big rain, we'd go to the hillsides below the mine road and pluck mostaza fresh from the damp earth?

And how back in the kitchen, you'd rinse the mustard greens clean and cook them in bacon drippings for lunch?

Then we'd sit at the small table, you, Grandfather and I, to eat the greens along with boiled beans and homemade tortillas, chatting about this and that between bites.

I sure miss those days.

I miss those winter mornings, before daybreak, when outside it would be so cold the dog's water bucket would be iced over, but inside the kitchen hummed with warmth from your cooking.

On the stove, MJB coffee boiled in the old coffee pot, the one with the glass knob in the lid so you could see the coffee perking.

I'd pour coffee into a thick mug, and lighten it with PET evaporated milk and a couple of spoonfuls of sugar.

"How would you like your eggs, boy?" you'd ask. "And how many do you want?"

"Couple of fried eggs would go great," I'd say.

I can still hear you cracking the egg shells against the rim of the cast iron frying pan that someone had dropped years before, breaking the handle off.

As the eggs sizzled and popped in the bacon grease, you tweedled out of tune while turning the eggs over with the metal spatula bent to just the right angle for scooping eggs without breaking yolks.

Then you'd set the plate in front of me. Thick slices of slab bacon. Potatoes fried crisp with bits of onion. Refried beans. Two eggs dappled with salt and pepper. Two tortillas. Fresh salsa. Bottle of Pepsi.

And Gramps would walk in with an armload of kindling for the living room fireplace, and you'd fry his eggs as he got that fire started, setting his plate in front of him when he was ready for breakfast. Finally, after serving everyone else, you'd sit down to eat.

For as long as I can remember, Gram, you've always put others ahead of yourself.

You've raised four children, and now, a passel of grandchildren and great-grandchildren, depend on you as well.

It's got to be trying.

I have memories of you in midsummer, in a limp pair of slacks and a sleeveless cotton blouse, standing at the kitchen counter, rolling out tortillas with a floured wine bottle. The afternoon heat streamed through the open doors and windows, and perspiration beaded on your brow and upper lip, but you labored on.

There was no sending out for pizza back in those days.

I can even remember you laundering clothes with a scrub board and a bar of Fels Naptha soap, heating the water in a wash tub over an open fire out back.

When it was clear the family wouldn't make it on what Gramps could earn, you got a job at the Fallbrook Hospital, scrubbing floors, changing linen, dumping bed pans. Your kids wouldn't go hungry, even if it meant sore feet and an aching back.

But now the years have caught up to you, and you're laid up in bed, your back tormented by arthritis, your stomach queasy, questioning all food.

"I'm tired," you say.

No doubt you're tired. You have a right to be tired. You've worked hard for 82 years.

I gotta think that sometimes, in the middle of the night when sleep won't come, self doubt must invade.

Did my existence have meaning? Did I make a difference? Was I worthwhile? Let me answer for you: YES! YES! YES!

Some of my earliest and best memories are bundled up with you. When I was 3, you used to bathe me, and stand me on the toilet seat, and sing to me in Indian while toweling me off.

When I was frightened as a child, I slept in your bed and you described how your mother went to heaven right after she died. To this day I can see her ascending on a cloud.

For every meal cooked, for every scrubbed shirt, for every washed dish, for every night you worried about me, for every time you made me laugh, for every memory you've bestowed, I say thanks.

I love you Grandmother, now and forever. Please get better.

These Days, The World Is Much Emptier

In the yellowed snapshot, she's 16 and sassy.

She's sitting on the rock wall in front of the Pala Mission, her black hair bobbed like a 1920s flapper, her eyes afire with the promise of youth.

In the next photo, she's 17, and standing in the overgrown yard of a ramshackle Pala Indian Reservation house. In her arms she holds a baby, my mother, and her eyes have changed somehow, a little less of the world-beater in them. Comes from changing diapers, I guess.

But then, that's life.

Tuesday, about 6 p.m., her lifeless eyes fixed on the ceiling, staring with all the expression of a goldfish floating belly up in a dime store bowl.

But then, that's death.

My grandmother, Delfreda Veronica Magee, crossed to the other side that night, and my world will never be the same.

It's the close of an era, an end to our time together.

Toward the end, I sensed she wanted to go. She was always a strong woman who cared about her appearance, and I'm sure the way the cancer ate away her body depressed her.

I know it depressed me. It's no picnic visiting a loved one who's shrunk to the size of a pin-feathered nestling. Seeing her too weak to get out of bed, little more than brittle sticks held together by loose flesh, broke my heart.

Her mother died of stomach cancer before her, and it was always my grandmother's greatest fear to die the same way.

But she died with grit, meeting the cancer head-on, even vowing to beat it. There are some battles, though, that can't be won.

For a couple of weeks my Aunt LeeAnn slept in my grandmother's bedroom at night, monitoring her breathing, making sure she didn't die alone.

My aunt and my mother and my cousin, Shelley, pulled bathing and cleanup duty, all doing what they could to keep her comfortable.

It was hard on everyone, including my uncles Copy and Peanut, who felt powerless to keep death from taking their mother.

Prayers helped. When you walked by her bedroom, you could hear murmurs of "Hail Marys," and "Our Fathers" from the elders and others gathered for the death watch. We brought straight-backed chairs in from the kitchen so people could sit while they worried their rosary beads and prayed with my grandmother.

She died with her own white rosary beads in her hands.

I left shortly after she died. I didn't want to be there when they slammed the door of the funeral-home van with my grandmother inside to drive her away to some dingy basement where they could work on her.

They did a good job, though. Friday night, when I viewed her in her casket, her cheeks were rouged and she had a dab of lipstick on her lips. Open your eyes, grandmother, and we can step out for Chinese dinner, I thought to myself. Crazy thoughts.

Saturday morning, I sat in the front row of the Pala Mission with the other relatives for the funeral Mass.

Red ribbons streamed like blood from the nail wounds in Jesus Christ's hands on the big crucifix hanging from the mission's crossbeam. Below it, my grandmother's gray casket waited.

The choir sang old mourning hymns in Spanish, songs that grab you by the heart and choke you, because you've heard these songs all your life and you know they mean death.

After the Mass, a procession of hundreds of people followed behind the Cadillac hearse along the road to the graveyard. It would be my grandmother's final graveyard trip, a trip made countless times to put fresh flowers on my grandfather's grave and to scold him for leaving her alone.

Now they are reunited.

Before they buried her, the people filed past to say their last goodbyes, some making a silent Sign of the Cross, others bending to give her a gentle kiss on the forehead.

"Adios, Adios, Adios," the choir sang, and cries of grief mingled with the dirges.

Too soon, there was the muffled thud of dirt hitting the concrete outer-box as men shoveled from the soft mound next to her open grave.

I shoveled too.

For Richer Or Poorer, Couple Bound By Love

People around these parts called him the Mad Russian, but he wasn't from Russia.

In fact, the closest he ever got to Russia was a shot of vodka now and then.

But his shock of white hair and unruly full beard made him look Russian, so the nickname stuck. His real name was Roy Foster. He was married to Camellia. And this is their story. A story of quiet love.

Roy was a barrel of a man. He was 6-foot or so tall, and carried 250 pounds or more of muscle and beer belly on wide shoulders.

I'm not sure where he hailed from originally. Probably Arkansas or Tennessee or West Virginia - one of those states anyway where they might say, "Could jya'll pass de'm taters?" with lots of twang.

They lived off Highway 76, on the eastern most corner of the Pala Indian Reservation, near Agua Tibia Creek.

Their simple wooden house offered little in the way of conveniences. Indoor plumbing was added somewhere along the line, but the place wasn't wired for electricity. No, it wasn't a fancy house, but it was their sugar shack all the same.

They shared the house with a fat Cumberland spaniel, as wide as he was long.

When Camellia cooked, she always made extra for the dog, and it ate and lounged in the living room until he was as round as some of the hogs Roy raised.

True to his origins, most days Roy wore bib overalls and white T-shirts, appropriate attire for his line of work, which was doing just about anything as long as it didn't involve a big paycheck.

He had one good paying job in his life, and that was when he worked in the labor union pouring concrete for a bridge right outside his house in the late 1950s.

But that didn't last long. He said he quit because he didn't like the surplus Army truck the boss made him drive to carry tools.

But I suspect he quit for a different reason. I think Roy simply couldn't stand being away from Camellia for so long each day.

Because from then on, Roy and Camellia were joined at the hip.

In all the years I knew them, I can't remember them ever being apart. In my whole life, I've never met two people closer to each other.

Roy was gruff and gravel-voiced, but always talked nothing but honey to his Camellia. And Camellia was loyal to the bone.

"It's you and me against the world, babe," Roy would say.

Once Roy and Camellia, who liked their beer, quit drinking for 15 years. The abstinence ended, however, one Christmas Eve. That night, fueled by booze, Roy picked a fight with Jean Jackson, a friend of his.

"I'm bigger and stronger than you, and I'm going to choke you," he told Jackson.

"You may be bigger and stronger, but I'm not going to sit here and let you choke me, Roy," Jackson replied.

As they went outside to settle the dispute, Jackson grabbed a baseball-sized rock from the rock garden and held it in his fist. When the Mad Russian charged, Jackson bloused him right in the nose with the rock.

Roy went down with a broken nose, but didn't stay down.

"Three times he came at me," Jackson said.

That's when Camellia jumped in and cut Jackson in the cheek with a kitchen knife. She wasn't going to let anybody beat up her man.

The incident soon passed, however, and they all stayed friends to the end.

One day, while driving in Fallbrook, Camellia's car was hit by a wealthy woman putting on makeup and not watching where she was going.

Seriously injured, Camellia spent several weeks in the hospital. Roy went crazy with worry. Couldn't eat. Couldn't sleep. Even the dog lost weight.

But Camellia, determined not to abandon Roy, pulled through. Afterwards, they got a sizable insurance settlement, the first time they ever had any real money.

They bought a mobile home in Fallbrook so Camellia could be closer to the doctors. But they hadn't even figured out how to work the new TV when Roy's eyes bugged out and he clenched his chest.

Roy died of a heart attack. Camellia died of a broken heart a short time later.

As Spirits Of The Old Ones Dance, We Sing

A gossamer mist, soft and wispy, billowed from the branches of scrub oak and tamarisk as spirits of the night breezed by.

And the night sky, made starless by drifting clouds, seemed somehow expectant, waiting for some kind of deliverance.

On this night, 30 of us gathered in a small clearing at the foot of Hot Springs Mountain and stared out at the shadowy landscape, looking at nothing in particular, mostly listening to dead calm.

Then gourd rattles broke the silence, shaking out syncopated rhythms; and voices led by Leroy Miranda Jr. sang Cupeno bird songs, songs not heard by these mountains for some 100 years.

We had come back to Kupa, our ancestral village at Warner Springs in north San Diego County, for a night of song and sweat to pay homage to the old ones who preceded us in death here.

Once this had been our land, where we birthed our children, prayed to our Creator, suffered our injuries, celebrated our triumphs and died our quiet deaths.

The hot springs here had been our power, the wild game and plants our sustenance. Our lives and this land were one.

But in 1902, we lost our land in federal courts. Seems we didn't have proper title, even though we had been on this land for as long as anyone could remember.

33

Governor John Gately Downey, who took over this land from John Trumbill Warner, who got it from the Mexicans, who got it from the Spanish, who grabbed it from the Cupenos, had plans for the land. His plans didn't include a bunch of red-skinned squatters messing up the place.

So in May 1903, armed soldiers encircled the thatched-roofed adobe homes and ordered people to pack what they could into mule-drawn wagons and leave. Simple as that.

Women wailed, babies cried, men resisted as best they could, but eventually most complied, except for the disconsolate few, who in fist-shaking rage, fled into the mountains, never to be heard from again.

It was a 40-mile trek from Kupa, down to their new home on the Pala Indian Reservation. To this day, Cupenos refer to it as the Trail of Tears.

And so we came to Kupa on this night to honor our dead.

Cans of Prince Albert tobacco, painted gourd rattles, bamboo clackers and a small hide-covered drum rested gently on the dirt mound at the sweat lodge's entrance. A short staff topped with an out-stretched eagle's talon and two eagle feathers wrapped with red yarn stood guard over it all.

We smudged our bodies with smoke from dried sage, and one by one filed into the sweat lodge, the womb of Mother Earth.

Hot rocks, glowing red from the fire, were placed at the lodge's center, and the canvas flap was lowered.

The sweat leader, Tubby Lavato, poured water carried from the nearby hot springs onto the rocks. The rocks hissed, and the steam smelled of sulfur.

First came the prayers, offerings from the heart. Then came more songs, voices raised in reverence to the old ways and the old ones.

After an hour or so, the rocks were spent. So another batch was brought in, and the ceremony continued.

The heat was stifling, legs cramped, backs ached from leaning forward. But it was good to suffer for the people.

Sweat flowed in rivulets from the body, spilling into the sand to mingle with the blood, sweat and tears of our forebears.

When it was all over, we toweled off by the fire.

"It has always been a dream of mine to have a sweat up here," Miranda said. "It sure felt good." "I know what you mean," said Lavato. "I could see them, the women in long dresses, the men in white shirts and Levis, dancing and laughing. I think we made them happy," Lavato said.

Plates piled high with a meat and potato stew and fry bread were passed around. And the talk was quiet and the laughter gentle as we feasted.

From where we sat, we could see the cemetery below, where wooden crosses marked the graves of long-dead Cupenos.

Rest easy, my people, you have not been abandoned.

Halloween High Jinks On The Rez

Shortly after World War II, back in the days when the Pala Indian Reservation had no telephones, TVs or sewer pipes, outhouses lined both sides of the village lane known as "Toilet Street."

Most of the outhouses on the San Diego County reservation are long gone now, replaced by modern plumbing, but a few still stand in quiet testimony to the days when the people were tough as mailmen, braving thunderstorms, howling winds and the dark of night to answer nature's call.

These were days when money was tight, and store-bought toilet paper was a luxury few could afford. Instead, Sears' catalogs performed double duty as reading material and outhouse wipes. Of course, the glossy pages were always last to go.

Heavy foot traffic cleared weeds from the path to the outhouse so stickers and bull thorns were few, but free-roaming chickens often left gooey surprises for those who chanced a trip barefooted.

I've been told that stepping shoeless onto a chicken pile at 3 a.m. in the middle of January is one of life's great thrills.

But then again, in those days, thrills were harder to come by.

Outhouse tipping was another cheap thrill - especially on Halloween night.

The way it worked, a couple of mischief-makers, hardly able to contain their giggling, would sneak up to an outhouse, and give it a good shove. "Timber," they'd whisper, as the outhouse teetered. Then a loud crash would disrupt the night as the outhouse landed, and angry people might start yelling from inside the house. Meanwhile, the boys would laugh and sprint off.

It became tradition for some people to keep an all-night Halloween vigil to safeguard their outhouses. Newcomers, however, were often caught off guard.

Which brings us to the Halloween, when a trio of young bucks (who shall remain nameless) decided to move outhouse tipping up a notch.

While celebrating with a jug of bootlegged wine, inspiration struck. Instead of just tipping the outhouses, why not drag them off a ways?

So, in the middle of the night, with a strong rope in hand, they crept up in an Army-surplus weapon's carrier to the corner lot on Toilet Street, lassoed the outhouse, hitched the rope to the truck's rear bumper and drove off with the outhouse in tow.

Over the truck's engine noise, it was difficult to hear anything except laughter.

But as they dragged the outhouse, the sound of a bellowing human voice became unmistakable.

"Stop the truck," one said.

"What's the matter?"

"Listen."

From the outhouse came a great outpouring of Spanish cuss words crackling like sparks from an arc welder.

"What the heck?"

"Cut the rope, Old Man Miguel must be in there!"

The boys had picked an indiscreet moment for their prank. Miguel, the Mexican farmer who recently rented the corner house, was caught in the outhouse with his pants down.

The boys cut the rope, then made a quick getaway without Miguel knowing for sure who it was that had him tumbling down the road in his own outhouse.

Now, Old Man Miguel may have been a simple farmer. But he wasn't that simple.

With two beautiful teen-age daughters at home, he figured the boys would be back. "Where there is honey, there will be flies," he thought.

So Miguel devised a plan for the next Halloween.

That night he moved his outhouse over a few feet. Then covered the open hole with twigs and burlap. On top of that, he spread a few shovelsful of dirt.

He stepped back to look over his handiwork. In the darkness of night, his trap was undetectable.

Nothing to do but wait.

Sure enough, in the wee hours, they came. Miguel could make out three shadows skulking toward the outhouse.

Then abruptly, there were only two shadows, and an excellent yowl filled the night.

Miguel stepped out into the yard with laughter of his own. There in his pit, was a youth knee-deep in outhouse muck.

And revenge never smelled so sweet.

A Peek Through A Grate Door At Wronged Ghosts

With afternoon sun glinting off its back, a narrow-bodied spider crawled on slender legs up the white-washed jail wall, angling toward its web in the shadowy eaves.

As I watched the daddy longlegs creep home, I couldn't help but wonder what it must have been like for the people locked up inside. With no windows, and a tin roof, they must have baked in summer and frozen in winter. For freedom-loving Indians, it must have been hell.

Measuring boot heel to boot toe, I stepped off the jail, judging it to be 25 feet long and 13 feet across, with a steeply pitched roof and concrete walls more than a foot thick.

Inside, prisoners slept in two cells on wrought-iron cots that folded out from the walls on short chains.

I don't know whether anyone knows for sure, but most say the jail was built behind the Mission San Antonio de Pala by the Bureau of Indian Affairs shortly after the Cupeno Indians arrived in Pala in 1903.

They might have needed someplace for uncooperative Indians still seething over being evicted from Cupa, their ancestral village near Warner Springs.

Celia Lattin, 81, said her stepfather, John Ortega, who was alive during the move from Cupa, told her that back then that Indians couldn't leave the reservation without a pass issued by BIA agents. If you left without a pass, or didn't return by the time your pass said you'd be back, you could be jailed.

She also said that a man who stayed out all night with a woman could be jailed by Indian police unless he agreed to marry her.

King Freeman, 61, says his grandfather, Race Freeman, came out from Mission San Luis Rey in the early 1900s for a Corpus Christi fiesta, and ended up in the jail for staying out with Martha Regetti, a woman he knew from his mail route. They soon married and had many children.

But more often, the jail was used as a holding tank for rowdies.

"I guess you could say it was a way to keep the peace," said Danny Portillo, 74. "If they caught you drinking, especially at fiesta, they could throw you in there."

Until the law changed in the early 1950s, it was illegal for Indians to drink or even buy alcohol. Some even went to federal prison for possessing liquor.

But where there was a will, there was a way.

On fiesta nights, some guys might pool their money and jump into an old jalopy to bounce up Pala-Temecula Road, which was dirt back then, heading north to the county line where a couple of Italian winemakers would sell them homemade wine, $1 a gallon.

If they stayed cool and hid their wine, the Indian police usually wouldn't bother them. But they would go to jail if they made trouble.

Celia remembered one night when she was about 17, there was a commotion as Bernardino Couts, one of the Indian cops, unloaded a couple of prisoners.

"We snuck up and peeked through a hedge to watch," Celia said. "I looked close trying to figure out who it was going to jail, then I realized it was my boyfriend, Fred Magee, they were locking up."

Fred Magee was my uncle. My grandfather, Paul Magee, also no doubt spent a night or two in the pokey, as well as a good many other reservation men.

Remijio Lugo, one of the Indian cops, used to arrest his own son, Tony, on occasion.

Usually, the men would sleep it off in the jail, and the cops would let them out the next morning.

They stopped using the jail in the 1940s. Roy Lattin, 74, who was an Indian cop in 1946 and '47, said they had stopped using the jail by the time he joined the force.

As the story goes, Alex "Spider" Garland kicked his way out through the tin roof of the jail and escaped, only to be caught an hour or so later down at a ballgame. After that, the jail didn't seem to have the same aura of punishment as it once did.

Today, the priest uses the jail as a storage room. But I can remember as a kid walking by the jail, peeking through the steel grate door into the dankness and being spooked.

On Sunday, the Pala Mission celebrates its 180th Corpus Christi fiesta. You might want to stop by for some good chow and check out the old jail for yourself.

Searching For Solace

Some days, when the blues hit, I trudge down to the San Luis Rey River bottom in search of solace.

Down there, my footfalls whisper on dry sand, and my running shoes mingle with the spindly toed tracks of roadrunners chasing lizards.

In the late afternoon, as the sun dips and the shadows stretch to full length, the wind often kicks up, carrying hints of brine from the Pacific. These breezes shuffle through the head-high willows and through the taller cottonwoods, until the shiny leaves almost tinkle.

Then the wind angles through the trees, and the tinkle changes to a sad wail, like the cry of a child lost in a department store.

When I get the blues, I feel like that mournful child, forlorn and frightened.

Mostly, when I get the blues, I feel alone. I'm not talking loneliness. That's something else. Loneliness is rooted in the absence of people. Like when your girlfriend or wife walks out, and you're eating pork chops for one. That's loneliness. Or maybe your kids won't give you the time of day, and you sit there wishing the phone would ring with a simple "Hi, Dad," or "Hi, Mom." Or maybe you're holed up in an old folks home, arthritic legs warmed by a pastel afghan, and your only company is Wink Martindale hosting some inane TV game show. Well, that's loneliness too. A craving for human companionship.

I rarely feel loneliness. Everyone has a different threshold for loneliness. Some people need a constant stream of people in their lives. These are social creatures who need conversation the way a junkie needs a fix.

I'm not that way. A little human contact goes a long way, for me. In fact, I more often crave solitude. I have to be by myself now and then to keep in balance.

This aspect of my character has caused me many problems over the years. People, especially my wife, think me rude when I seek isolation. It's difficult for them to understand that my need for seclusion equals their need for interaction.

So, loneliness isn't one of my problems. No, when I say alone, I mean something apart from loneliness.

The alone I'm talking about is a kind of spiritual abandonment.

You see, I believe all of us must seek a benign liaison with the spiritual order or life-force of the cosmos.

Divine providence apportions each of us our measure of life-force, and it's up to us to keep it linked with the mother lode.

When I am doing right, when I'm walking the good road, living in harmony, I am spiritually strongest.

But when I stray, when I put my life off kilter with shoddy habits or selfish wrongdoings, my spiritual strength diminishes.

It's at these low ebbs that I feel emptied of spirit, abandoned and unconnected to the collective spirit. That's when I feel most alone, adrift in the cosmos, severed from purpose or meaning.

I realize this is heady talk, and boring to some, but I'm just trying to explain what the blues feel like to me.

My blues come in other guises, too.

Life can be harsh, the fates cruel. The English author Thomas Hardy called them purblind doomsters, these tricky henchmen of destiny who place nails in the road that blow out tires, causing you to slam into a tree.

When bad things happen, I get the blues.

Sometimes I get the blues just looking at my hands. I no longer have a young man's hands. Wrinkles and rough spots decry my age.

And I'm reminded of my shortcomings. I fret about my life, and all that I haven't done. All my unfulfilled dreams. All the challenges sidestepped. And am awash in self-pity. I get the blues.

So I walk in the river bottom, listening to the wind, wallowing in the blues.

You can't always be cheerful, I tell myself. It's good to have the blues. The lows make the ups that much higher, I say. It's all part of the human condition.

And I walk on. And eventually, I feel better.

Sand Trap Kept Fun Afloat For Yesterday's Kids

Reservation cats are safe when the weather's like this, far too hot for dogs to move.

By midafternoon, with the sun on full flame, the dogs sprawl in the shade, unwilling even to twitch a green-bodied fly off a limp ear, let alone chase some stupid cat.

The Pala Indian Reservation lulls in the summer heat. Mongrels snore. Bored kids sit with their backs to eucalyptus trees and talk in undertones. Unconvincing breezes drift through dry leaves, rattling them like bleached bones in a soothsayer's cup.

At the Pala Mission, the spongy parking lot asphalt feels like warm flesh underfoot. Brash sunlight angles across a white wall where a blue-bellied lizard clings to rough plaster. Bees fuss in the upper reaches of pepper trees. Sparrows chirp in lackluster voices.

Hot day.

When I was a kid, on days like this we hung out at the Sand Trap, a concrete ditch about 30 feet long, 4 feet across and 5 feet deep, filled with water.

To this day, I don't know what exactly the Sand Trap was, but I believe it was part of the reservation's drinking water system. I know grown-ups didn't like us swimming in it, but it was out in the brush, near the banks of the San Luis Rey River, so most of the time we could get away with it.

The water was cool and clear enough to see crayfish skulking along the sandy bottom. Part of the fun was to

45

dive for the crayfish, trying to pluck them up behind the claws to keep from getting pinched. Pretty fast underwater, they were hard to catch.

I remember that when I was about 8, I hung out with my cousin Robert Banks, who was about 13. He was my idol.

He slicked his hair back and had enough wave in the front to make a decent jelly roll. My own hair was arrow straight, and any attempts to imitate his hair ended in a spiky, porcupine look.

At the Sand Trap, we'd have contests to see who could swim underwater the longest. He, of course, always won. After another easy victory, he'd haul himself out of the trap and stretch out on a towel. Next to him was his pack of cigarettes.

He smoked Kools and even had his own lighter. After knocking a cigarette loose from the pack, he'd flip open his Zippo with one hand and fire up, exhaling through his nose in a cloud. I used to think, what could be cooler than that?

Sure, there were other boys around who smoked at 13, but none who was actually allowed to smoke. My Aunt Martha even used to buy him cigarettes. Back then, she didn't know cigarettes were bad. None of us did.

I'd watch in awe as he smoked his cigarette down to the filter, then flick the sparking butt airborne in slow twirling arc into the sand.

Sometimes, after a day of swimming, we'd go rabbit hunting before dark. Bullets were expensive and sometimes we'd leave for a hunt with only five shells apiece.

Robert was a great shot. I was with him when he nailed a jack rabbit in the head at a dead run from about 50 yards with an open-sighted, single-shot .22-caliber rifle.

For fun we'd throw cans in the air, and he could plink them out of the sky every time. For targets we used Lucky Lager cans. The red "X" in the middle of the can served as a bullseye. We'd set the cans up on a fence and shoot till we ran out of bullets.

I haven't been hunting with Robert in more than 30 years. He's married now and has a family. Me, too. I wonder if he can still shoot? Wonder if I can still shoot.

Well, the Sand Trap is gone now. Covered up, I guess. And HUD houses now occupy the best places where the rabbits used to run.

But the heat is still here. And the kids are still here. Only I think we've messed it up for today's kids. There just isn't much for them to do on hot days on the rez any more. I see them sitting listless on the rock wall in the park in front of the mission. Baggy clothes. Backward caps. Bored looks.

I wish the Sand Trap was there for them.

An Old Soldier In The Process Of Fading Away

One unremarkable morning, nearly 30 years ago, the sun yawned in a faded, cloudless sky. No wind bothered to blow the dust off the pepper-tree leaves. Even the green-backed flies, usually zipping about, seemed listless, lingering too long where they lighted, becoming easy prey for the swatter.

Half-blind with cataracts, Salvario swiped at the blurry flies with a rolled-up newspaper.

"Whack!" And a fly turned into a bloody smear on his khaki pants. He flicked the winged remains off his khakis with a tobacco-stained fingernail.

Salvario Chavez, also known as Sarge, always wore khaki, Army surplus khaki. World War II, a war he was proud to paratroop in, left an indelible imprint on his fashion sense. After the war, he left the Army, but the Army never left him.

In the mornings, Sal liked to warm up in the sun, sitting on a straight-backed chair near the front door of his Pala Indian Reservation shack.

Two rooms built of thin slats, the shack held only his bed, a wood-burning stove and a small table. By day, the windows, as filmed over as Sal's eyes, allowed in little light. By night, flames from the cooking fire illuminated the bare room when Salvario lifted a lid from his stove. He seldom wasted money on lamp kerosene. Money was better spent on wine.

In the wee hours, the fire would die and the house would be cold in the mornings. His war wounds ached in the chill, so he sat outside and waited for the sun.

Come 7 a.m., slanting light dodged the pepper tree enough to spill warmth over him. His skin oiled up in the heat. He scratched at the white cheek stubble that was nearly as long as his close-cropped hair.

Across the dirt road from him was another shack called the "Black Castle," where Guido Moro stayed.

On that long-ago day in front of the Black Castle, the previous night's fire lay in ashes. Empty chairs and upturned orange crates circled the ashes. Empty wine bottles, dented beer cans and mashed cigarette butts littered the ground.

Guido raked up the bottles and cans - dead soldiers he called them - into a pile off to the side.

Sal couldn't see that far, but he heard the rake. It wouldn't be long, now. From a coffee can at his side, Sal pulled out a bag of Bull Durham tobacco and a packet of rolling papers. He held a paper, slightly folded, between his left forefinger and thumb, sprinkling in tobacco flakes to roll a smoke. He thumbnailed a kitchen match to spark the cigarette's end. Acrid smoke plumed from his wide nostrils as he exhaled.

Jerome Garcia, an irregular at the Black Castle, was first to arrive. Sal heard his "Tallyho," greetings to Guido. The time had come. Sal took hold of his cane to stand on swollen feet. His military Oxfords were scuffed, dirty and untied.

Jerome, a beer drinker, came with a six-pack of Lucky Lager under his arm. Sal preferred wine, but beer would do in a pinch.

He reached out for the beer Jerome handed him. It was warm. A habit picked up while stationed in England, Jerome liked beer warm and often set it in the sun to heat.

No matter, Sal punched open the tin can with a church key and swallowed. First drink of the day. First drink of the rest of his life.

Like ringing a dinner bell, the opening of beer cans called the others. Soon, the Jackson brothers, Pat and Ross, got there, as did Carl Siva, Peanut Magee, Victor Smith, Fernando Ortega and more. Like Sal, they're all gone now, except for my Uncle Peanut.

But on that day they drew a circle in the dirt, and tossed in their change. "No rat-holing," they chided. My Uncle Peanut walked to the store with the money, and returned with a half-gallon of Tokay, "Old Tokyo."

He cracked open the bottle and handed it to Sal for the first shot. A token of honor. Sal tipped the bottle, and pulled deep. His milky eyes watered when he lowered it.

Sal settled into a chair. Finally warm, he started his stories: "Back in the war, when I hit the silks, I screamed like an eagle. They called me `Screaming Eagle.'" "Ah, the only silk you hit, was jumping from sheets to sheets," someone teased.

Thus began the day's talk. A day like any other.

Hot Salsa With Peppers Great On Chili Days

In the cultural mix that is Southern California, Indians and Mexican Americans share a common history. Thrown together by circumstance a couple of centuries ago, they often worked side by side - tending cattle, hoeing row crops, harvesting hay.

Over the years, friendships formed. And with human nature being what it is, intermarriages ensued. As a result, the two cultures overlapped.

Many Indians of my grandparents' generation spoke three languages: Indian, Spanish and English. In that order.

In those days, Indian people learned Spanish not in the classrooms, but in the fields. Spanish even became a way for Indians of differing dialects to communicate. While English is the dominant language for Indians today, the imprint of Spanish remains strong.

I, for one, am extremely happy the two peoples met, for out of their alliance came a great boon to Indian life - the chili pepper.

Sunday, I honed my favorite knife on a rat-tail sharpening steel in preparation for making salsa. (Don't ask me why, but many Indians pronounce it sar-sa.)

"Always make sure your knife is sharp, boy," my grandfather used to say.

First, I sliced five fat yellow chilies lengthwise, then diced them up small crosswise. I did the same with five serrano chilies.

There's a satisfying crunch as the blade chops through the chili skin.

Years ago, after my grandfather's legs got too weak to do much, he took over the salsa job. He had an old kitchen table and some chairs set up in the shade of a big tree in front of his adobe house. In summer, with Pacific-borne breezes cooling the afternoon, he and I would sit under the tree, drinking beer and cutting chilies.

Too poor to travel much in his life, when he did go to a far-off place it stuck in his memory. And as we worked, he liked to tell of a trip to the eastern Sierras outside Bishop, when he packed in with a Paiute buddy to catch trout in mountain streams. He often talked of the cold water, the snowy mountains and the big fish, repeating the story like a mantra.

As he talked, his hands, dark and leathery, took care to see the dicing was precise, so no big chunks spoiled the texture. It took him a long time to make salsa. But I'm convinced the time he invested made it taste better.

These days, I could put salsa makings in a food processor and have it ready in seconds, but I don't. I cut the chilies the way my grandfather showed me, by hand.

With the chilies done, I cut five or so fresh tomatoes into small cubes, then add half a diced purple onion, chopped cilantro, a clove or two of minced garlic, fresh lime juice and salt to taste.

In my grandparents' house, no meal was eaten without something hot to go with it. Even for breakfast, my grandfather gummed (he had store-bought teeth but hated to wear them) a jalapeno with his oatmeal, toast and coffee.

Now and then, my grandmother liked to make a different kind of salsa by grinding dried red chilies and garlic in a metate, a stone bowl, then spooning in tomato sauce until the consistency was right.

Then she'd fry up chorizo, onion and eggs in a cast-iron skillet and we'd make burritos with homemade tortillas, drizzling on her salsa. Bite into that and you'd first get the fresh tortilla taste, then the spicy chorizo and egg mixture, and finally the hot sauce kicked in to heat up your whole body. Pepsi on ice was a good way to cool off.

Every year I promise to grow my own chilies, but every year I end up bumming from other rez gardeners. He's dead now, but I liked Chicken Rodriguez's yellow chilies best. They weren't scorchers, but had plenty of flavor. I liked them for lunch. A bite of chili, a bite of salami and cheese sandwich, a sip of beer. Good stuff.

If we couldn't get them fresh, we'd eat pickled chilies from a jar with hamburgers. Or in restaurants, where there was nothing else, Tabasco sauce on eggs-over-medium and home-fried potatoes. Or red chili flakes on pizza. Or hot oil on Chinese food.

As you can tell, I like it hot.

Goodbye To Quiet Man

The old rugged cross atop the Pauma Indian Reservation chapel leaned sharply to the west. A mottled brown sparrow alighted on the cross, surveyed the crowd, then flitted off.

Saturday, hundreds of people, far too many to fit inside the jammed chapel, stood beneath pine and pepper trees out front. Out of respect, men removed their hats. Women shushed their children. Rez dogs avoided fights.

Inside, the Rev. Paul Macroni said the funeral Mass for Samuel Joseph Powvall. Traditional Spanish hymns lilted through open doors and windows. Sniffles and muffled sobs punctuated the sad verses. Sam would be missed.

By today's standards, Sam lived a small life. Except for his time overseas in World War II, he spent all his 76 years on the Pauma reservation in North San Diego County. He didn't dine with kings. He didn't disco with movie stars. He didn't crave gold chains or Italian suits.

He wore jeans cinched with a tooled-leather belt, T-shirts in summer and flannel shirts in winter, a good Stetson hat and cowboy boots.

He worked in civil service for many years at Camp Pendleton, retiring in 1976. He provided for his family. He fed his horses. He took out the trash.

Yes, he lived small but, in a big way, with quiet dignity.

Few people knew Sam was a war hero. His Army unit, pinned down by enemy fire, looked done for. German troops, led by tanks, advanced. But Sam rushed from concealment, charged a tank, dropped a grenade down its hatch, then commandeered its machine gun to beat back the enemy.

His medals for heroism included the Bronze Star and two Purple Hearts. But Sam was tight-lipped about it. He didn't hold with boastfulness.

For years, he served as tribal chairman for the Pauma Reservation. And, too, he gave countless hours to the Indian Health Council board.

He was chosen to lead his people, and he exercised his responsibilities with modest wisdom, never a heavy hand.

I first met Sam more than 25 years ago, when his son Ronnie and I stumbled into his kitchen after a full night of carousing. It was about 4:30 a.m., but Sam was up and you could smell the coffee.

Seeing our inebriation, he wordlessly poured us steaming mugfuls, and pointed to sugar and a can of evaporated milk on the table.

The three of us sat around his breakfast table, drinking coffee and talking. In Indian country, it's regulation to tell elders your parentage right off. It gives them a way to place you. So I filled him in.

"So you're Paul Magee's grandson, huh?" he said.

I nodded.

"Come outside. We can talk while I feed the horses."

In the half-light of dawn, he threw flakes of hay to two horses corralled out back. He talked to them, patting their necks as he filled the old bathtub he used for a trough with water. He loved horses.

In a half-hour or so, he would leave to round up cattle with his son Chuckie for friends on the Santa Ysabel

Indian Reservation. My plan was to drive down the hill and sleep all day. I felt like a bum by comparison.

I watched him finish his chores. He moved easily, a short but powerful man, built like a squat draft horse.

But toward the end, life bent Sam's back. He endured the loss of far too many loved ones: two sons; a daughter; a granddaughter; his wife, Margaret; and many other friends and relatives.

Each death chipped away at Sam, stealing his joy of life.

Sam was godfather to my first-born daughter, Tyra, so I would visit him now and then to hear stories of his life and times. He spoke Luiseno fluently and knew much about the old ways.

For his death, he chose the very old way of cremation instead of a casket. Down at the Pauma graveyard, beneath the shade of an old pepper tree, they lowered the Indian pottery bowl that held his ashes into the grave. On top of the ashes, they placed his boots and favorite Stetson.

"Rest easy, compadre. Ride with your buddies across the sky," I thought as I helped shovel dirt into his grave.

Sweating It Out On The Way Home

In the last 30 or so years, I've celebrated five Thanksgivings with my parents. I'm driving up to San Jose this Thanksgiving to make it six.

By the time you read this, I should be at my mother's kitchen table sopping up the last of my breakfast eggs with a flour tortilla. My mother fries her eggs in bacon grease. They're very good.

There's a certain sense of finality to this trip. After 30-some years in their home, my parents are planning to sell and move to Idaho. This may be the last Thanksgiving in their big house. I want to be there, and I want my kids to be there, to share the day with them.

Before leaving for the trip, I called King Freeman and asked if we could sweat Saturday night at his lodge. A sweat is a good place to pray for a safe journey. "Sure, let me call Doc and we'll get things going," King said.

When my son Bear and I got there, Randall "Doc" Majel was starting the fire. To properly heat the rocks, you need a good bed of hot coals, so I grabbed an ax and split chunks of eucalyptus to feed the flames. When the fire was right, we threw in 25 or so river rocks - blue ones are best - then covered them with more wood.

With the chores done, we sprinkled a mix of tobacco, sage and cedar on the fire to ask for its blessing, and unsheathed our gourd rattles.

Doc has been teaching me Bird Songs, beautiful old songs that, if done in the complete cycle, can take days to sing. The songs describe the migration of the ancients as they looked for agreeable places to live. Today they are performed at social gatherings - fiestas, pow-wows and parties - for fun.

A while back, I bought a rattle from Joe Guachino, an elder Bird Singer who lives on the Morongo Indian Reservation. He frequently comes to Pala for funerals and other Indian doings. He's a friend.

About 20 years ago, Joe hollowed out a grapefruit-sized gourd, hardened it in boiling water, dropped palm seeds into it, then glued in a handle he had whittled from cottonwood.

It became his rattle of choice. But after Joe acquired a new rattle, one with a bigger sound, I proudly bought his old one.

I thought that since Joe had rattled with it for so long, it would know all the beats by heart. Not so. Well, maybe it knew them in Joe's hand, but in mine, it forgot everything.

Now, I can sing. But when I try to rattle while singing I feel like Steve Martin in "The Jerk," like a guy who can't clap and stomp his feet at the same time.

Some day I hope to sing with my sons. Brandon, my 15-year-old son, sings with his buddies and they're quite good. They've been learning from Robert Levi, one of the real masters, and they are often asked to perform at other reservations.

Meanwhile, I sit by a phone that never rings with invitations for me. So I practice the Bird Songs with Doc, hoping some day, maybe ...

On Saturday night, after a short while Lawrence "Onnie" Mojado walked into the firelight. And King arrived, too. We smudged with smoke from dried sage and crawled into the lodge, the womb of Mother Earth.

As doorman, I scooped up the glowing rocks from the fire with a pitchfork and carried them into the lodge's center. Then I crawled in. Upon word from Doc, the sweat leader, I dropped the blanket door into place and the sweat began.

A rule of the sweat states that what is said in the sweat stays in the sweat. But there is also time for silent prayer, so I said prayers of thanks:

I thanked the Creator for my loved ones, for it is only through their love that I am a complete human being.

I said thanks for a body that carries me along the trails where my ancestors also walked.

Thanks for a mind that allows me the consciousness to connect with the cosmos.

Thanks for the mystery of life that keeps me guessing as to how it will all end.

And thanks for being old enough to turn down the lime Jell-O layered with cream cheese and dates that my Mom used to force-feed me on Thanksgivings past. I always hated that salad.

Homemade Tortillas

Back in the dark ages before women's liberation, Indian men used to joke about keeping their women barefoot, pregnant and home makin' tortillas.

They don't joke anymore. They pine for the days when women made fresh tortillas.

Maybe I'm wrong, but I can't think of one Pala Indian woman under 30 who makes tortillas regularly. Most are horror-stricken at the prospect of tortilla dough stuck beneath their acrylic fingernails.

I fear the art of tortilla making is going the way of 8-track tapes, double-bladed razors and virginity before marriage.

Used to be, fresh homemade tortillas accompanied every meal. Women would rise before dawn to knead dough for the day's tortilla supply. Heady aromas of boiling coffee, frying bacon and fresh tortillas filled Indian kitchens.

Today's Cap'n Crunch mornings seem bland by comparison.

Since the death of my grandmother several years ago, I've had to subsist on store-bought tortillas. While OK, store-boughts lack the moist, lardy lusciousness of homemades. You can't taste love in a store-bought.

I yearn for the long-ago mornings when I sat at the kitchen table, rubbed sleep from my eyes, sipped coffee lightened with evaporated milk and two sugars, and watched my grandmother make tortillas.

With wisdom acquired from her mother, she'd work dough in a big mixing bowl, adding flour, water, baking powder, lard and pinches of salt in unmeasured, intuitive proportions.

She'd dust a cutting board with flour, lift the dough from the bowl and let it plop on the board. Then she'd dust the blob and knead it some more, slapping it like a baby's behind for good measure.

She'd tear off fistfuls and roll them into dough balls, flatten one with her palm then attack it with her rolling pin. Her rolling pin was really just a length of closet dowel worn smooth as a creek pebble after years of use. It was her favorite. But she could roll with anything. I've seen her use a quart wine bottle with equal effectiveness.

She'd finish shaping the tortilla by hand, stretching it to a near-perfect, wafer-thin round. With her cast-iron grill searing hot, she'd throw on a tortilla, let it slightly blister, then flip it using thumb and forefinger. She'd do this several times to assure even cooking, then toss the tortilla into a bowl lined with a dish towel.

Once she'd made about a dozen, she'd set the bowl on the table. I'd peel back the dish-towel cover and steam would rise from the stack. I'd grab one, rip off a piece, wrap it around a piece of bacon, dip it into egg yolk spiced with salsa, and sink my teeth into ecstasy.

Tortillas added intrigue to all my favorite dishes.

When the cactus leaves were young, I'd go across the San Luis Rey River, harvest a bucketful of the tenderest leaves I could find, clean them of spines and present them to her. She'd dice them and sprinkle them into chunks of steak browning in bacon grease with onions and garlic. She'd top it with a tomato-based chili sauce and let it simmer.

She'd serve the steak and nopales with fresh pinto beans boiled in ham hocks, hot salsa and homemade tortillas. Man, oh, man.

She did a similar thing with spareribs, browning them first, then simmering them in chili sauce. You could suck the meat right off the bone, and the sweetness of the tomatoes and the heat of the chili cartwheeled on the taste buds.

Sometimes she'd boil short ribs in a broth of salt, pepper, bay leaf and other spices until the meat was tender. I'd dip bits of meat in mustard, saving the delicacy of the marrow till last. I ate that with tortillas stuffed with mashed avocados sprinkled with lemon juice, salt and pepper.

But those days are gone forever. I never get fresh tortillas anymore. And it looks like the only way I'm going to is to make them myself. It's not easy. I've tried. Every tortilla I've ever rolled looked like a map of Texas. And I don't have the ingredients right. Fifteen minutes after leaving the stove, they get hard as crackers.

But I'm going to keep trying. I don't want to spend the rest of my life tortilla-less.

Grandfather's Jeans Gene No Longer Fits

My grandfather, Paul Magee, was a Levi's 501 type of guy. No matter the weather or the occasion, he buttoned on a pair of 501s.

In summer, the dogs shed, the birds molted, but my grandfather never, in my lifetime anyway, wore a pair of shorts or bathing trunks or anything else that bared his legs. Oh, in a swelter, he might peel off his red-plaid flannel shirt to catch the breeze in his old-man, slingshot T-shirt, but he never exchanged his jeans for anything cooler.

When we went to the beach, he sat jeans-clad in the sand, gumming fried chicken and sipping Lucky Lagers. A desert Indian, most at home amid the sage and the cactus, ocean water held no sway over him. He didn't body surf, Boogie board or hang 10. I doubt he could swim. He preferred not to get his jeans wet.

My grandfather usually owned two pairs of jeans. Frequent scrubbings in the washtub out back faded his every-day pair to the color of an Australian shepherd's eyes. He reserved the newer, dark-indigo pair for dressier occasions.

Sundays, he'd belt on his new jeans, button his shirt to the collar, cinch his bolo tie and tilt his white Stetson to a rakish angle.

In the Pala Mission, you could hear the stiff denim whisper with each step as he made the long walk to communion. After Mass, he'd linger outside for a time, roll a Bull Durham and have a smoke with the menfolk.

Then he'd change back into his old jeans, hanging the Sunday jeans in the closet where they stayed until the next week. Comfortable, he'd head out for the day's adventures.

In his prime, my grandfather broke horses in his jeans. He carried downed deer out of the back country while wearing jeans. He chopped the wood that heated the house while wearing jeans. He sat on orange crates and told stories by firelight in his jeans.

I knew the end was near when, after his stroke, my grandfather abandoned his jeans for sweat pants. His jeans defined his life. They were part of who he was. What he was. To give them up meant surrender. Too weak to button his jeans, my grandfather never had a proud moment in sweat pants.

Sometimes I feel like I'm betraying his legacy, now that I don't wear 501s. They used to be my favorite pants, too, but things have changed.

Years ago, 501s seemed to fit better. With wear, they would soften to form-fit the contours of my posterior.

I'd step into the jeans, button the 32-inch waist and feel encased in comfort.

But, like I say, things have changed. The last pair of jeans I bought were size 38s. And now they're two sizes too small. I have to inhale until my navel touches my spine to button them. And, tight as they are, they still don't stay up.

So, Gramps, I apologize for not carrying on the jeans tradition. But you can see why I'm wearing khakis.

Indian Pride And The Generations

I'm not sure exactly when it happened, but sometime around the turn of the century, some Southern California Indians grew ashamed of being Indian.

It's understandable. I look at newspapers of the era, and read the many descriptions of Indians as dirty savages, unfit for polite society. Society wasn't polite to Indians back then. And, surely, some Indians felt second class.

I believe this shame became most pronounced in my mother's generation. But I saw signs of it in my grandfather's, too.

As a young boy, I remember walking into a San Jose church with my grandfather, holding my hand. My grandfather, always a quiet, reserved man, seemed to pull even further into himself around non-Indians, and that Sunday we slipped into church, trying to be invisible.

Afterward, I overheard my grandfather mention to my mother that he felt good because I was not ashamed to walk beside him in church.

"Why in the heck would I be ashamed? What did I have to be ashamed about?" I wondered.

I found out later, when my mother told me stories of her youth, of being made to sit in back of the Oceanside movie theater because her skin was dark.

Because my father is white, I'm light-skinned so I haven't suffered the prejudice that my mother has. But I know that my mother, and many of her generation, wished out loud they weren't Indian.

65

Both my maternal grandparents spoke Indian. But they didn't teach any of their kids to speak it. My grandparents' generation felt it would be best in the long run for their children to learn the way of the whites.

It was in the 1930s and 1940s that much of the Indian language died in Southern California. Initiation rites, the indoctrination to Indian religion ceased to be held. The whirling, dances, the funeral image ceremonies, the eagle rituals - all ended. Peon, the traditional game played at fiestas, dwindled to a few players. Bird songs were nearly forgotten.

In the 1950s, the Bureau of Indian Affairs introduced relocation programs, offering inducements like free vocational training and help with housing if Indians would move to big cities like Los Angeles.

Assimilation was the watchword then. By weaning Indians from reservation life, Indians would simply get stirred into the melting pot.

With Indians in the mainstream, reservations would dwindle and eventually the bureau could terminate them.

But the radical 1960s saw a resurgence in Indian pride. Hippies admired the noble savage, and this appreciation spread to other sectors of society. Indians felt validated, and Indian pride surged throughout Indian Country.

Indian cars, beat-up old boats, boasted shiny "Red Power" bumper stickers. The American Indian Movement shook its fist at America and demanded Indian rights. Armed with lawyers instead of lances, Indians battled for sovereignty.

Thankfully, there were some elders who held onto the old ways. In the 1970s, they taught classes in Indian language, basketry and herbal medicine. In tribal rooms across Southern California, elders sang into tape recorders, so new generations could learn the songs. Elders supervised the building of sweat lodges, and prayers, once nearly lost, could be heard again on reservations.

My generation played a part in bringing back respect for the old ways.

And our kids grew up with Indian pride. They wrote it on their school binders. They tattooed it on their arms and ankles with India ink and needles. They carried it with them in the way they walked.

But now my generation is having second thoughts. We worry that our teens are becoming too full of Indian pride, at the expense of learning about the rest of the world.

Our teens have grown up with each other. They hang out with each other in school. They party with each other after school. They live a full-on reservation life - isolated and insulated from the rest of the world.

Now, like my grandfather's generation, my generation wonders if that's such a good thing.

A Fiesta Frame Of Mind

Recently, my son Bear and I shot hoops at Pala Park in Temecula.

As I showed him how to roll the ball off the fingertips, how to arc it toward the back of the rim, how to ascend to the basket with body control, the sun beat down on my shoulders.

And the sting of it felt good. It felt so good, it put an Indian guy like me into a fiesta frame of mind.

In the past, say a hundred years ago, Indian people put great stock in fiestas.

The old people, my grandparents included, told stories of bouncing along the dirt roads in the back of horse-drawn wagons as the family traveled for days to attend a fiesta.

Back then, a fiesta lasted a full week, maybe even two. Families built ramadas, coverings of willows or palm fronds, that served as restaurants in the front and sleeping quarters in the back.

At long-ago fiestas, the people raced horses, climbed poles, played a game called peon, sang Bird Songs and danced, and the young at heart no doubt found time for hanky-panky.

I guess I went to my first fiesta as a boy back in the 1950s. They held it down in the sandy flats by the San Luis Rey River, where the sewer ponds are now, on the Pala Indian Reservation.

For kids, fiestas were something else: Running around barefooted, in cutoffs and a dirty T-shirt, playing tag on the grounds, throwing rocks at your cousin who called you names.

Grown-ups paid you no mind. As long as you weren't bleeding, anything went. Fiestas meant freedom.

Nobody called you home for dinner. When hungry, you ate bean tortilla rolls from ramadas. When thirsty, if you had a dime you bought a pop; if you were broke, you drank cold water from the faucet. At night, when you got too tired to run around, you found a warm spot by the peon fire and fell asleep curled in the dirt.

I didn't become a full-fledged fiesta-goer until the late 1960s. I was a teen when I discovered what fiestas were really about.

Fiestas put the real world on hold. They suspend reality. They erase yesterdays and tomorrows, leaving only the fiesta moment.

Fiestas have a similar feel in all Southern California Indian Country. Whether it be in Barona, Rincon, Santa Ysabel, Campo, Pechanga or Soboba, the fiesta has commonality.

Like the smell of ground beef and onions sizzling in a cast-iron frying pan. Like the Indian woman in a flowered house dress, standing in old tennis shoes with no laces, rolling out tortilla dough. She throws it on a griddle, lets it blister then flips it over.

Old-timers in cowboy hats gather at tables in the ramadas and drink coffee lightened with sugar and evaporated milk, smoke unfiltered cigarettes and eat slices of pie made with commodity peaches.

Seventeen-year-old Indian girls, as pretty as any God put on this good Earth, circle the grounds in packs. They put on proud, haughty looks along with their lipstick and eye shadow and dare you to give them the eye.

They wear jeans and cowboy boots, or white pants and sandals, or shorts and halter tops and their silken black hair flows to their waists.

The band plays oldies and people dance. And there is much laughter. Eventually, some guy with too many beers mashes his potatoes too hard and hits the floor. He bounces up, like nothing happened. And there's more laughter.

When the band stops, and the dance ends, the singles trickle toward their cars.

It's a Fats Domino kind of night, with stars winking in an indigo sky. In Indian talk, it's snagging time.

You lower the tailgate on a pickup truck and convince the girl you've been dancing with all night to have a beer with you.

And after some talking, if she likes you, she'll sit beside you.

And elsewhere you'll hear some guy say, "Git over here," to some girl. And somewhere else you'll hear "Stop it" and then a laugh, from some girl.

And James Brown plays on eight-tracks and you wish the night would never end.

The sun on my back brings fiesta nights back. Some of the best nights of my life.

A Writer is Cramped

When I was a young writer living in my grandmother's house on the Pala Indian Reservation, one problem was finding a place to write. I couldn't write in my room. I slept in a screened-in back porch with my Uncle Peanut. There was barely room there for our Army bunks and the water heater.

Certainly no place for the desk, bookshelves and other trappings I envisioned a writer needing.

Besides, my Uncle Peanut's lifestyle didn't mesh with the writing life. Back then he was a wino. At 3 a.m. he'd be nipping his bottle and smoking a Kool. At 5 in the morning his buddies would bang on the door with offerings of peppermint schnapps. By the time I got up, I was dog tired from not sleeping.

Back then, I had never met a real writer, but I knew many had fine places to write. I used to check out books from the Pala Bookmobile on my favorite writer, Ernest Hemingway, and had admired photos of his Cuban writing lair.

I read all of the famous scribe's works that I could get. I knew he often wrote dialogue standing up. But he also had a desk. And floor-to-ceiling bookcases. And stuffed African antelopes on the wall. Most of all, he had solitude. I envied Hemingway's solitude.

At my grandmother's house, if it wasn't my uncle bothering me, it was the nieces and nephews who were always underfoot.

To try to get away, I set up my portable typewriter on the kitchen table. It was a ghastly table, a lime-green veneer on wobbly, cast-iron legs, but with the kitchen's doors closed, I could write there.

My young writer's eye danced with imagery for short stories and novels, but before I could finish typing a thought, my grandmother would shuffle in to bang some pots. When she couldn't think of something to talk about, which was seldom, she hummed. About the time she finished, my grandfather would take a coffee break from cleaning the yard and sit down and chat.

"Boy, Fernando must have tied one on last night," my grandfather would say with a small degree of envy. Fernando was one of his drinking buddies. "Did you hear him? He roared like a lion this morning."

Even back then, I wanted to be a famous writer. But to get famous, I had to write undisturbed.

I talked to my grandmother about needing a place to write. She suggested I go see Aunt Martha, who might have a room in her old house.

So I did. Shortly after World War II, the government gave away surplus military homes called Linda Vista homes. If Indian people had a mind to, they could go to San Diego, tear down a house and reassemble it on the reservation.

But the homes were shoddily constructed. The plyboard was paper thin. The windows rattled and cracked in the wind.

The house behind my Aunt Martha's was a Linda Vista house. She stored stuff in it. I had to crawl over old tools, bikes and chairs to get to the spare room. Junk filled it, too.

"Clean this room out, and you can use it," my Aunt Martha said.

I chose not to. It looked nothing like Hemingway's study in Cuba. Spiders lurked in every dusty corner. Maybe I should have taken the room. Maybe I could have launched my writing career from there. Maybe. But I doubt it.

Although my grandmother never said so, I think she wearied of this strange, monastic kid camping in her kitchen, pounding away on the typewriter.

Why don't you clean out a room in your mother's house out back? she asked.

My mother, too, had a Linda Vista house out back. My Uncle Peanut used to talk about sleeping in it. Then I found out he slept under it.

I went through the house. It brimmed with junk as well. I spent much of the day going through old boxes. I found papers from my great-grandfather in there. Notations in neat script. But I ran out of gas before I was done.

I never did get a nice place to write - a room of my own, with a desk and book shelves and trophy game on the walls.

I joke that it was all that stood between me and fame.

Goodbye To A Homer-Hitting Shortstop

Wispy clouds shaped like horsetails drifted through a flat, turquoise sky. A young girl in sandals held an umbrella over her grandmother's gray head to shade her from the hot sun. Older men in cowboy shirts and straw hats smoked quietly outside the fence.

In the old Cupa graveyard behind the adobe chapel at Warner Springs, I stood next to Susanna Blacktooth's grave. She died in 1968, while I was still in high school.

On this day we buried Robert Lavato Sr., 77, a friend from Pala.

I guess Robert Lavato, or Bobby as most called him, was most famous for being the son of Roscinda Nolasquez, who was born in 1892 and had memories of life in Cupa, the Indian village at Warner Springs. She remembered the eviction in 1903, when the people were forced to leave their homes and travel by wagon to the strange land of Pala. But then that's another story.

Bobby was born in Pala, but chose to be buried near his mother in the old Cupa graveyard. Dressed in his dark-blue Navy uniform, Bobby reclined in the satin-lined coffin, old photographs of family life pinned to the lid.

His open casket rested before a concrete cross in the graveyard, with hundreds of people gathered about.

As a procession filed by to pay final respects, some made a sign of the cross, some lightly touched his lapel, some stood and prayed in the Indian language, invoking the Creator to help Bobby on his spiritual journey.

According to custom, Bobby's clothes were burned a couple of nights before the funeral. A hole was dug in the back yard of his mother's house. As singers lifted their voices heavenward and dancers imitated birds in ritualized steps, Bobby's clothes were incinerated. Dancing flames lit the faces of people clustered around the hole.

An Indian's possessions have always been burned after death. I've been told the burnings dissuaded spirits of the dead from coming back for their things. Long ago, when houses were little more than grass huts, whole houses were burned to fend off wandering spirits. But when houses got more expensive, practical matters superseded and houses were no longer torched. I think the last house was burned in Pechanga in the 1930s.

I sat Friday night in Bobby's velorio, or wake. Inside the Pala Tribal Hall, bolts of cloth covered the walls, especially the windows and the doors. The materials kept unwelcome spirits out. People in folding chairs faced Bobby's casket. Flames flickered from candles in pewter candlesticks. Flower arrangements and wreaths bannered with words like "Goodbye Uncle Bobby" fanned out from either side of his casket.

Up front, Katherine Siva Saubel and Robert Levi sang Cahuilla funeral songs, their voices punctuated with rhythms from shaken gourd rattles.

Sitting there, I recounted some of Bobby's accomplishments. From 1954 to 1960 he served as tribal chairman for Pala, fighting against termination. He worked 30 years for the sand and gravel operation on the reservation. He fathered 10 children.

Once, when I was in a gym in Temecula, I met a guy, Augustine Ferdy, who asked me where I was from. When I told him Pala, he wanted to know if I knew Bobby Lavato.

Sure, I said.

Ferdy went on to tell me how Bobby was the best athlete he ever saw. He was best known on the reservation as a baseball player, a homer-hitting shortstop.

At the funeral, I ran into Lloyd Arviso, 80, from Pechanga, the best softball pitcher ever to come out of Indian Country around here.

Arviso leaned back in the front seat of a Thunderbird and said, "I grew up with Bobby, played ball with him, drank with him. Now he's gone. All my friends are going."

As Bobby's son, Angelo "Tubby" Lavato, smudged the casket with smoldering sage, he prayed for his father. When the men lowered the casket into the grave, I grabbed a shovel and helped throw in dirt.

As I shoveled, I heard the wails of his grieving daughters. I wished them peace and I wished Bobby a peaceful hereafter.

Grin, Bear it, On Indian Time

Contrary to movie stereotypes of stern-faced, mute Indians wrapped in a blanket, propped against the wall of a fort, Indians are really gregarious people who love to laugh.

Go to an Indian home for a family gathering and you will find Indians cutting up, cracking wise and teasing. You see, teasing is almost an Indian national sport.

Indian humor is a complex cultural phenomenon. I don't want to write a sociological treatise here, but I thought it might be fun to share some insight into Indian humor.

For instance, there is the concept of "Indian Time." Indian time never fails to get a laugh with other Indians. It goes something like this:

Indians view the white world as a punctual one. They see mainstream males buying expensive, wafer-thin watches with alarms to make sure they're not late. And mainstream women in power suits take high-heeled steps down the sidewalk, repeatedly glancing at their wristwatches, hurrying to be on time.

Indians, however, are habitually late. Maybe the inclination toward lateness is changing these days as Indians assimilate more into the power structure, but traditionally it's been hard for Indians to be on time. I'm banking things haven't changed that much since I worked in Indian business 25 years ago.

For instance, let's say you're due at a 2 p.m. Indian meeting to argue with some water-company bureaucrats

77

who don't want to pay the tribe for downstream water rights.

To get to the meeting, first you need to fire up the old war pony, your 1973 Buick Electra with the "Indian Car" bumper sticker.

You know your car needs a battery, but it costs $60 for a new one, and you just spent your last money on taking this beautiful Indian girl to a Redbone concert. What's more important, a new battery or "Come and Get Your Love," Redbone's 1970s hit? That's easy. Love is better than a battery any day.

So you go out to your car, cross your fingers and turn the key in the ignition. Sure enough, it's dead. Dang it. You walk the dirt road to find your uncle to jump your car. No problem, though. Judging from the angle of the sun, you've got two hours before the meeting's set to start.

Your three dogs follow. Down the road a bit, four other dogs jump out and a brawl ensues. You holler and try to pull your dogs from the fray and some dog bites your hand. Now you've got a puncture wound between thumb and forefinger.

You turn around for home. You pour alcohol into the tooth wound and it burns like heck. You don't have any Band-Aids, so you Scotch tape some toilet paper over the bloody hole. It'll hold at least until the blood dries. You head back to your uncle's.

No problem. Still plenty of time. You find him pulling weeds in the garden out back, and he says, sure, he'll jump your car. You climb in his blue, 1956 Chevy pickup and head over. At your car, you feel under the front seat for the screwdriver. With the flathead end, you pop open the trunk and grab the jumper cables.

The cable wires are frayed in places, but they've always worked before. You hook them up to the positive and negative posts, while your uncle does the same to his battery.

You try the key. No fire. You wrap some duct tape around the cables. And this time they work.

After unhooking the cables your uncle drives off. You run into the house for a fresh T-shirt.

You're late, but judging by the sun, not that late.

You drive the 50 miles to town, stopping every now and then to pour another quart of cheap oil into the crankcase. So the Buick burns a little oil. It still runs, don't it?

The parking garage costs $7 and you only have $4. So you park six blocks away and hoof it. You pass a clock in a store window and it says 2:30. Dang. The meeting started a half an hour ago. You pass another store window and there's a Redbone poster on the wall. Wow. And it's only $3. You go in and buy it.

It's 2:45 when you walk in, poster under your arm.

"Sorry, guess I'm on Indian time," you say.

The Indians all laugh. They know all about Indian time. They were late, too.

Thanksgivings Past Fondly Remembered

In my mind, I'm still a kid. I see through 16-year-old eyes, even if they do require reading glasses now. I look to adults to steer the boat, while I daydream of faraway places.

From the kitchen of her adobe house on the Pala Indian Reservation, my grandmother captained Thanksgivings. I was simply along for the ride.

She'd start early in the morning, mixing flour and water for tortilla dough. I'd walk into the kitchen to see her fingers sticky with dough.

On such mornings, I'd spread butter onto a warm tortilla, pour a cup of coffee, sweeten it with evaporated milk and sugar and get the heck out of there.

It was either that or get steamrolled by my grandmother as she hurried from pot to pot, turning up heat here, turning it down there, stirring, turning, tasting.

Turkey wasn't enough for my grandmother. Usually, she baked a ham. And better yet, she often fixed spareribs in a mole sauce. First she browned the ribs in a cast-iron skillet, then simmered them in the tomato-based mole until the meat practically fell off the bone.

Mashed potatoes, of course, were a staple, with flour and water whisked into turkey drippings for the gravy. Beans, too. We always had pinto beans, boiled with ham hocks, so the beans could sop up that smoky, porky flavor.

My grandfather made the salsa. He'd sit outside with a small cutting board and an old paring knife and dice jalepenos with small, tight slices. While my grandmother hustled about the kitchen, he took his time, preparing the salsa with precision. Sometimes, I'd sit with him, and listen to tales of his young life after his mother died, when his father sent him off to live with his aunts on the Cahuilla Reservation.

He told me of cutting and carrying wood for the cookstove. Of carrying water for baths. Of hiking through the brush country, hunting for rabbits. His aunts spoke only Indian, and he learned to speak Cahuilla there.

"They were good to me," he said, his lazy eye glazing over with memories.

In the early afternoon, aunts and uncles and cousins would arrive, bringing more food — pies, cakes, candied yams and such.

Little kids sat in the living room, seated around the coffee table. Adults gathered around the wooden dining-room table. My grandfather sat at the table's head, near the hutch covered with statues of saints, near the old bronze clock with the horse rearing at its dial. My grandmother, when she did sit, took the chair to his right.

My grandmother was famous for dry turkey. I believe she was so insistent on having everything ready on time, she carved it too early, and it sat too long.

In later years, she took to steaming the sliced turkey in an electric roaster oven until serving time. Much improved.

Good humor spiced the table talk. Stories about my Aunt LeeAnn as a young girl, sitting atop a department-store motor scooter, twisting the handle and going "vroom-vroom," or trying on new shoes in the shoe store, then dancing for the clerk to show him they were good for dancing.

Or my Uncle Copy would talk of playing baseball for the Army in Germany and seeing Elvis in uniform there. Most of my Uncle Peanut's good stories had to do with his drinking days and weren't fit for the dinner table.

Besides, he preferred eating to talking at Thanksgiving, always the first to dig in for seconds.

With the last of the pie gone and the dishes in the kitchen, my Aunt Vivian would shuffle over in her bedroom slippers for a cup of coffee.

"Ah, here comes the Queen of Hearts," my Aunt LeeAnn would say, and we'd break out the cards and play nickel-dime-quarter poker into the night.

Time has taken those great Thanksgivings from me. My grandmother and grandfather are dead.

Now, I'm the grandfather. And though I wear adulthood like an ill-fitting suit, I realize it's my turn to steer the boat. My turn to make memories. Here's hoping for good ones.

24/80   Harvey   ROBERT FREEMAN

Christmas At A Slower Pace

I've been in downtown San Francisco, where passers-by donned sunglasses against the glare of Macy's Christmas lights.

I've seen honey-haired women in pearls, cashmere sweaters and leather trench coats hurrying down sidewalks, shopping bags thumping against their knees.

I've felt the night vibrate as celebrants bustled to the next Christmas party.

But Christmas has a different tempo on the Pala Indian Reservation. Slower, quieter, tiptoeing in on moccasined feet.

Maybe Christmas this year has dimmed amid the millennium hype. I don't know, but much of Pala seems laid back about the holidays.

While wandering around the Pala Mission the other day, I noticed the manger scene going up. Warped plywood formed the stable roof, but nothing else was done. Although nobody was working on it at the time, no worries.. It'll come together before Midnight Mass, I guess.

Years ago, Christmas had more fervor. Men in beat-up pickups harvested evergreens on Morgan Hill above the reservation, then passed them out to people in the village below.

Grateful folks offered the men beer, and they'd stop to talk, rubbing the pine pitch off their fingers while exchanging banter. Then they'd be off to the next house, where excited kids ran out to help unload. Later you'd see kids on front porches stringing together popcorn and cranberries for garlands.

But so much has changed over the years. Now I see even the mission has an artificial tree.

Sometimes I think like my buddy, Virgil Yazzie, a Navajo from Indian Wells, Ariz., who married a Pala woman after a stint in Vietnam.

"I don't believe in Christmas," he said. "We didn't know Christmas when I was a kid."

He grew up without a television, without electricity for that matter, and Rudolph the Red-nosed Reindeer was nobody to him.

"To us, Christmas was just a another day."

With no connection to Christmas, maybe Christmas is easier for him.

But for me, Christmas often rings hollow. I get the Christmas blues.

My cousin Tiffany has the Christmas spirit. She cajoled her old man into hanging up hundreds of lights on my grandmother's old adobe house.

Her mother, my Aunt Lee Ann, who lives behind her, also has a bunch of lights on the roof and interlaced with the branches of her front-yard shade trees. With all those lights, planes overhead can use them as navigational beacons.

I wander about the mission grounds, staring at purple devotional candles, and remembering the Christmases of yesteryear.

My grandmother loved Christmas. And without fail, she celebrated with tamales. I often drove her to a small Mexican market in Escondido where they sold her favorite masa, the corn-meal dough spread on corn husks that encase the chili-beef center.

Christmas Eve, her kitchen would be thick with tamale steam, pot lids clanging a tune when the water boiled high.

After Midnight Mass, we'd return to a tamale feast, red juices running down our chins and down our wrists.

As much as she liked Christmas, my grandmother had unusual gift-giving habits. Once I was of age, every year I knew my gift would be a six-pack of Coors and a carton of Marlboro cigarettes with a $10 bill taped to the box.

To be honest, I liked my gift just fine. But then, we weren't so health conscious back then.

I was recalling all this in wanderings, wallowing in my Christmas blues, when I happened upon my cousin Bubble-Up's grave. He died not too long ago, of a bad heart.

And I spotted, thumbtacked to his wooden cross, two handmade Christmas cards from his daughters.

One of them said: "Dad, this is for you. Merry Christmas and Happy Holidays. I love you Dad." The other also wished Dad a "Marry Christmas."

I pictured those two young girls, coloring those cards in red and green, and aching for their father on Christmas and instantly the meaning of Christmas hit home.

A Down Jacket Warms Memory

I'm writing this on Sunday, in my 18-foot trailer, where storm winds blow through cracked windows, jostling the jaundice-yellow curtains. On my ancient cassette deck, Miles Davis purrs "Kind of Blue" through his horn, unsettling my soul. The neighbor's mongrel, lying on the cushion outside, sighs through his nose because I won't come out to play.

My grandfather's black-framed glasses rest on the bridge of my nose. He died 13 years ago, but his glasses, with lenses ground from real glass, sit with substantial weight on my face.

I'm not sure why he wore them. He couldn't read well. He couldn't write at all, except to sign his name in an unsure slant. No matter, he thumbed through the newspaper now and then, gleaning what he could from news photos and box scores. But mostly he gathered info from news radio and talk shows. Then, later in the day, he could sit with his buddies, take a pull from a bottle of port, and talk knowingly of the world's goings-on.

Saturday, the electronic alarm sounded at 5 a.m. and I rolled out of flannel sheets into gray sweats for a run. From the closet, I pulled my grandfather's goose-down jacket off a hangar.

In all these years, I've never washed the sky-blue jacket. Sweat and grime from his neck and wrists stain the collar and sleeves. No, it doesn't look good, but then nobody ever accused me of fashion sense. And I only wear it jogging.

My mother bought him the jacket some long-ago Christmas. She knew of his occasional binges, when he'd pass out from too much wine in a chair in a friend's yard, or on the ground, or Lord knows where.

We never were a family to buy expensive, brand-name stuff. So the jacket isn't a North Face, or an Eddie Bauer, or an Abercrombie & Fitch. No, it's a Sears. But it's warm.

I imagine the jacket was my Mom's way of keeping the cold out of her father's bones. A way of allaying her fear that he might take sick with pneumonia and die.

I wear the jacket now, worry free. He rests for eternity in the Pala Mission graveyard. On his headstone is a photograph I took at one of my kid's birthday parties. In it he wears his jacket.

Now it's my jacket. I slip my arms into the sleeves and feel the loft of the down beneath the nylon. I remember that same feel, when I had my hands beneath his arms to hold him up, to steer him home, to get him safe in bed so I could sleep in peace.

My dog, Griz, greets me at the front door, his stub of a tail wagging. I give him the ritual petting, tell him he's a good dog, and we head out the gate.

Up the road a piece, the neighbor's sweet-faced, pit-bull terrier joins us. She comes over, smiling, and I give her a pat and tell her she's a good dog, too. And the two of them leap at each other, the way canine friends do, then bound off in synchronized motion.

I turn left on the graveyard road, the one that runs past my grandfather's grave and lumber on into the darkness. My jacket swishes as my arms move with my pace.

Moonlight illuminates the dirt road. Clouds, petulant with stormy thoughts, drift past the moon. More clouds, black like burnt mattress stuffing, streak overhead.

It's shadow time, no hint of first light. Leafless sycamore branches, luminous in the moonlight, claw like arthritic fingers at the sky.

The wind and the dogs cut through the brush. Twigs rattle, dead leaves crunch, and the dogs pant.

But the wind, carrying a chill and the scent of sage, can't get through my grandfather's jacket. It's zipped to my neck, and I'm warm.

A glittering of stars peek from holes in the clouds. Indians believe my grandfather is one of those stars. I imagine him looking down at me with Milky Way eyes, watching me, his grandson, running with the dogs in the dark in his old jacket.

In the Indian way, it's important to keep loved ones that have crossed over alive in memory. Don't want to forget the sound of his laugh, the warmth of his smile.

After all, despite his faults, my grandfather loved me. And that's all I ask of life — to feel beloved now and again.

In the Spring the Reservation Sheds Its Winter Coat

Spring arrives on the Pala Indian Reservation in an old-man's T-shirt.

On spring mornings, well before winter's daybreak, grandfather sun rises, tinting gray clouds with streaks of crimson. In the evenings, twilight dawdles for kids to do extra bike wheelies or to stand in front yards and gossip before darkness ushers them indoors.

Cottontails, invisible during winter months, appear like rabbits from a hat along sandy trails to nibble spring grasses. Hillsides, sere in summer, roll out the green carpet in spring. Leaves sprout on barren elderberry trees. Blossoms, pink and white, bloom on fruit trees. Lilac growing wild amid the sage and chemise, perfumes the air.

In the Pala village, foxtails, bull thorns and other unwelcome weeds congregate in yard parties, threatening to run amok. Power lawn mowers, rototillers and weed cutters buzz Saturday mornings in the war against overgrowth.

Forty years ago, men turned garden plots over with spades. Earthworms, severed in half by shovel blades, squirmed in winter-damp soil. Spring marked garden planting. Some folks bought tomatoes and chilies and green peppers in small containers from nurseries. The more adventuresome grew everything from seed.

In spring, men left their flannel shirts in drawers favoring instead the white, old-man T-shirts, the kind bought in three-packs from Sears or Montgomery Ward.

With brown arms unencumbered by sleeves they hacked down weeds with a grubbing hoe then tilled the soil with a garden spade. They lined out rows in the turned soil, creating spillways for irrigation water. They sprinkled seeds from packets bought at Poor Old Rube's, the grocery store preferred by Pala Indians shopping in Escondido.

They built fences of chicken wire and discarded 2-by-4s to keep the rabbits out of tender plants shooting up in mounded rows.

In the evening, men sat back in broken kitchen chairs with hand-rolled smokes and a tall cans of Lucky Lager to admire their handiwork.

Few Pala households bother with gardens these days. Not enough time. Too much work. It's so much easier to buy ready-made salsa in plastic containers from the deli.

The rhythms of spring have changed. In the old days, Georgie Machado, in Army surplus fatigues with a small cigar clamped in the corner of his mouth, tractored the weeds in the field around his house, discing them under. Smoke billowing from his tractor exhaust and smoke from his stogie were sure signs of spring.

Sylvester "Wedo" Diaz, until he was well into his 80s, hoed his garden in an old-man's T-shirt with a red bandanna knotted about his neck and a straw cowboy hat shading his nose.

And many reservation women planted flowers, petunias and geraniums and violets, in flower beds and clay pots and coffee cans. They kneeled in the earth, scraping the soil with a claw-shaped hand tiller, mixing fertilizer into the soil.

Few women plant spring flowers any more. It's so much easier to buy them already blossoming from garden shops in town.

Feeling the approaching heat, the rez dogs summerize by shedding hair that women sweep off kitchen floors along with tortilla crumbs, Cheerios and tracked-in dirt.

Feeling the approaching heat, folks hose off ice chests, washing out dirt and dust left from last summer's ballgames. Some find long-forgotten cans of beer rolling around the bottom. The ice chests will cool fresh cans at this year's ballgames.

As heat approaches, younger Indian women put away their sweat pants and change into shorts. And tank tops and curve-hugging blouses take the place of sweaters and nylon jackets.

And in spring, thoughts of Indian love mingle with the onset of peach and apricot blossoms. Young men play basketball shirtless on warm afternoons, and jump higher and shoot further than normal. And young women pass by and laugh a little louder and walk a little slower in hopes of catching an eye.

And in the warmth of a spring sun, even the old men's chests seem to swell a bit while guts get sucked in beneath the white, old-man T-shirts.

In The Stands For Improved Ramona Pageant

For as long as I can remember, my mother has been telling everyone she can corner how her father was a cousin to the famous Ramona.

We kids would fidget in the station wagon while Mom regaled the gas station attendant about Ramona while he pumped gas and squeegeed the windows.

I'd elbow my little brother, "There she goes." And we'd brace for the lengthy story while cars idled behind us waiting for a fill up.

The Ramona thing is a running joke among us kids. But for her, it's a serious fascination. One she never tires of. When I've run out of gift ideas for my mother, a nice, Ramona-related gift will always work. One year, I bought her a leather-bound, turn-of-the-century edition of Helen Hunt Jackson's novel. Another year, a Ramona video.

Mom loves all things Ramona. Once, we drove to Old Town San Diego just to see where Alessandro and Ramona married.

I reminded her: "Mom, these are fictional characters." It didn't matter. We had to wander the adobe hacienda where the storied marriage took place.

For 77 years, the Ramona Pageant, a spin-off of the novel, has been performed at the Ramona Bowl in Hemet. But I never went. Never wanted to.

Long ago, I read "Ramona." That was enough for me. I wasn't drawn in by the sentimentality, the melodrama, the frilly skirted romance of the story. While I admired Jackson's desires for reforms, for her vehemence over the dishonorable treatment of Southern Californian Indians, couching it in a fictionalized, overwrought love story didn't work for me.

I'd also heard stories, about the cheesy campiness of the Ramona production, the dime-store Indian headdresses, the drug-store beaded moccasins, the pale-faced pretend Indians in wigs, and I didn't want to sit there and squirm in embarrassment.

So I stayed away.

But lately, the Indian grapevine reports a changed pageant. New sensitivities have spurred attentiveness to cultural accuracy. Local Indians have been invited to perform. And Cahuilla and Luiseno culture count for something in this evolving pageant.

Now, I was curious.

My son, Brandon, came home with news that he and his peon (Indian hand game) team had been invited to perform in the pageant. And my daughter, Missy, had been asked to dance with the Bird Song group.

On Sunday, the Pageant Association sponsored an Indian VIP day, inviting many local Indians to see the improvements. I got my invitation in the mail and I decided to give the pageant a try.

After 77 years of improvements, the Ramona Bowl is quite a showpiece. The hacienda, resembling the adobe ranchos of early California, occupies center stage.

Climbing roses, palm tees, flowering shrubs splash the landscape with color. Ascending hillsides form the bowl, with trails winding through the granite outcroppings and native brush.

Brushy Indian dwellings perch on hillside ledges along with a one-room adobe hut where Ramona and Alessandro live.

The stands hold about 5,000 people. And the cast of the pageant numbers about as many. That's an exaggeration, of course, but it's a huge cast, which requires several hundred volunteers to pull the whole thing off.

What made it most fun for me, was seeing the pageant with other Indians.

When we first walked in, a friend of mine, Benjie Magante from the Pauma Indian Reservation, announced like a circus barker, "Shade pills for sale. Get your shade pills here."

And we cheered and booed in the appropriate places.

Even the small improvements matter. For instance, the pageant brought in Ernie Siva, an expert in Indian music from the Morongo Indian reservation, to revamp some of the Indian songs. Now many of the songs are authentic.

And, I saw many old friends on stage, singing, dancing, rattling and it felt good to see that finally local Indians were being included.

Yep, I'm sending Mom pictures.

Summer Of Love With A Rusty-Red '48 Dodge Truck

Something in an Indian man loves a pickup.

In the summer of 1970, as I lay in bed listening to mosquitoes divebomb exposed flesh, I envisioned myself bouncing along dirt roads in a rez truck, my arm out the window, a load of firewood stacked in back.

Oh, I had had cars before, but they had been tame, citified cars, made for grocery-store trips and church on Sunday. No, an Indian needed a stiff-springed, big-wheeled pickup, the way an Indian of yore needed a war pony.

I conjured a truck where my dog could ride in back. Where I could throw a deer after hunting. Where I could put a mattress and sleep under the stars on fiesta nights.

One major obstacle, though, I had no money. How could I buy a truck with empty pockets? But fortune smiled and I landed a short-term job as a roofer's helper, laying red-clay tiles on the Pala Tribal Hall's roof.

Money — all $80 of it — itched for a truck after I cashed my first paycheck.

It was my cousin, Randy, who found it. He drove me to Lucio's dairy and knocked at one of the homes built for dairy workers. An older Mexican man in a white T-shirt and a pencil-thin mustache opened the door.

"Ah, so you're the guy who wants a truck, huh?" he said.

We followed him out to a graveyard for farm vehicles next to a big hay barn.

"Alla," he said in Spanish, pointing.

Glowing amid the rubble like a diamond set in coal sat my truck. The moment I spotted her I knew she would be mine. She was a rusty-red flatbed, a 1948 Dodge, with a near-flat rear tire, a cracked passenger window, and pigeon crap over roof and hood.

She was a beauty. She was freedom, prestige, thrills on four worn tires. Some kid had spray-painted white peace symbols on the doors, which only added to her charm.

With shaky fingers, I counted out $50 from my wallet and gave it to him. No papers changed hands. No registration, no pink slip, no bill of sale. No problem. Why sweat the details?

He found a tire pump, and as I worked the handle, I saw nothing but potential.

Why, if my grandmother bought a piano, I could transport it for her. And if I got a few head of cattle, well, I had a truck to haul hay. And who knows, maybe the priest might need to pick up a statue or pews from Mission San Luis Rey. I could volunteer my truck. Why, this truck might be my passport to heaven.

We hooked the truck to my cousin's Roadrunner with a long chain and towed it back to the rez. With my cousin in the lead, I steered along Highway 76, imagining the day when my truck would speed along on its own steam. Seat springs and stuffing poked through the worn spots in the upholstery. Black electrician's tape wound around the steering wheel. The rear view mirror was missing. But I grinned, hands at 10 and 2 on destiny's wheel.

With the remaining money I bought spark plugs, a set of points, carburetor cleaner, oil and some of that oil additive for old engines.

Shortly after I bought the truck, my job ended. So if anything big needed repairs, I'd be in trouble. The Mexican guy, however, assured me that with a little tender lovin' the truck would run.

In the shade of a pepper tree, with my grandfather's transistor radio blaring on the seat, I worked magic with borrowed tools, getting my truck in shape.

For weeks I toiled, pulling the oil pan, boiling out the carburetor, cleaning the engine. You could eat off that flathead six.

Finally the day came. With no money for a battery, I gathered neighborhood kids to give me a push. Heading along the down slope of Pala Road, I popped the clutch. Sputter, cough, wheeze.

"Keep pushing," I yelled.

Again, I popped, and with a few fits, the engine caught. I drove the truck for several delirious minutes before it died.

Dejected, I reparked it under the pepper tree. Out of money, out of time, out of luck, I accepted the $50 Auggie Norte offered for the truck, and headed back to college.

But for a few wondrous moments, anyway, I was an Indian with a truck.

...........Mission Bells Ring, Rez Dogs Howl Over Loss

Life unrolls, not like a red carpet, but like toilet paper thrown over a front-yard shade tree.

Leonard Siva, a friend, died last week. White corpuscles rioted in his bloodstream. Leukemia, the doctors decreed.

And the phone jangled. "Last chance to see Uncle Leonard," my wife's sister said. "The nurse gave him three hours." All along, it had been a matter of time. Now, time crooked its finger at him.

At the news, my wife and son raced to his bedside. I, however, didn't go. I ducked death. I avoided his shrunken frame beneath white sheets. I evaded his deathbed gasps. I eluded the a roomful of grief. I chose to live with better memories of Leonard.

An hour or so later, the phone rang again. "Can you ask Chuckie to ring the bells?" my sister-in-law asked. When someone of the Pala Indian Reservation dies, it's tradition to ring the mission bells. But not with the perfunctory ring that calls people to Mass. No, the death knell is a slow, rhythmic dirge, with heartache sandwiched between the clangs. And Chuckie is the one to do it. And the rez dogs, incited by the bells, howl. And the howls don't just call the wild, they lament. They pierce the sky with sorrow.

"I guess this means he died," I said.

"Yes," she said.

When I tell people I'm from the Pala Indian Reservation, the common reaction is: "How nice to live in a place where you know everybody."

And that's true. I see a guy walking down the road, and I know when he wrecked his car. I know when that kid fell out of a tree and broke his arm. I know when she snagged her prom dress on the floorboard nail.

But the knowing has a downside. I know the dead and the dying. Sometimes the knowing is too much.

Leonard and I shared the same birthday, Sept. 26. And though neither of us put much stock in astrology, there seemed to be similarities in our character that coincidence couldn't explain.

As a kid, he carried a schoolboy crush on my mother. He recalled holding hands with her in front of the mission.

"I could have been your father, boy," he liked to say.

And I'd just laugh, but inwardly I'd wonder who I'd be if he was my father. Would I recognize myself? Fortunately, we mortals can't answer such imponderables. But the question did arise.

I didn't really know Leonard until about 20 years ago. He lived many of his adult years in and around the Morongo Indian Reservation, where he raised a family. He returned to Pala later in life.

The night my grandmother died five years ago, Leonard showed up at my house with a cooler full of beer. And we sat at my dining-room table and drank until dawn.

The beer flowed, and our lives unfurled like an American flag. We talked of sports, of the sweetness of scooping up a hot grounder and rifling it to first. And the satisfying thwack when it popped into the outstretched glove. In Indian country, the Siva name is almost synonymous with sports, and though I never saw Leonard play, I'm sure he was a helluva ballplayer.

He talked of close calls in the Korean War, of gunplay and grenades and advancing tanks, of missing home, of friends he saw die, of the sense of loss every soldier feels.

Then we talked of my grandmother and his mother, Aggie. And the grief escalated to an out-of-control pitch and the two of us sobbed at the dining-room table, tears of loss rolling down our faces. But we felt no shame, no loss of manhood.

Leonard wore regret like blue jeans. He wished so much to have been a better husband, a better father, a better son, a better human. I, too, live with many of those regrets.

The night ended. Daylight ushered in reality, and we parted company.

I'm listening to the Texas Tornados as I write this. And in Leonard's idea of heaven, Tex-Mex is playing on St. Peter's jukebox right now. And Leonard's sitting down to a cold beer, and a plate of hot beans, chili meat and tortillas served up by Aggie.

It's been too long since he's tasted her cooking.

Picking Jojoba Seed Amid Life's Chatter

We're big Indians in a small Pontiac Tempest. I'm scrunched in a corner.

The radio doesn't work. No matter. Wherever Cool-City Carl Siva goes, Fats Domino's "Blueberry Hill," follows. He sits lowered in the front seat, eyes masked behind black Ray-Bans, hair pomaded to a slicked-back shine, big arm out the window, head bobbing to internal piano music.

We're riding low. We're not low-riders, but we're too much weight for worn shocks. Six of us in a car built for three Indians. Sparks fly when we scrape over bumps in the road.

My Uncle Peanut Magee steers the white steering wheel with the chrome horn bar. I sit behind him. His black hair streaks across a spreading bald spot. He sits wide-shouldered behind the wheel, smoking a Kool. He's poised to be the life of the party.

Brakes squeak for the stop at the Border Patrol checkpoint near Pechanga. A green-uniformed agent walks around the car, looking at us with suspicions. I hide an empty beer can beneath the driver's seat.

The mirrored-sunglasses stand at my uncle's window.

"Sir, what country are you citizens of?"

"Pala," my uncle replies.

We bust out laughing.

"Magee," Cool-City Carl says. "Pala isn't a country."

No, Pala isn't a country, but it's our world. It colors our vision, permeates our talk, haunts our night dreams. It will shadow us to the other side.

After some corrections, the Border Patrol allows us to pass. In the early 1970s, no red-roofed tracts crowd along Pala Road. We cross the old Pala Bridge, now torn down, and turn right toward Aguanga on Highway 79.

Even with the windows down, the car's red interior smells like honky-tonk — old booze, stale smoke, empty promises.

It's early. We could all use more sleep. Even Juggie's glass eye seems red with fatigue. We drive into the rising sun. Those without sunglasses squint.

Sleepy or not, the banter continues. My Uncle Peanut gets a roasting for his Border Patrol foul-up. And the road climbs, past Vail Lake, past Dripping Springs, past the corner where what's his name almost lost it coming back from the dances at Los Tules.

Granite boulders boil up from the hillsides like teen-age acne. Cholla cactus cast spiky, butch-waxed shadows in the sand. Near the Stagecoach Inn we spot the squat gray plants of the jojoba berry.

My uncle pulls onto a dirt road and we bounce along ruts and high spots until he feels we've gone far enough. We pile out into the summer heat, grabbing gunny sacks from the trunk. Jojoba bushes dot the hillsides along Temecula Creek.

Put your fingers around the shiny, acornlike jojoba seed and pull. Drop it into the sack. Find another. The more you pick, the more you make. The man from UCR will pay $1 per pound. Something about oils in the jojoba seed being like sperm-whale oil. The university wants to experiment. It's thinking, save the whales. We're thinking beer money.

Once a week, an old guy in a white pickup shows up in an Aguanga turnout. We turn the seeds in, he weighs them and gives us cash. Some weeks we make $100 or more each.

We grind on. Stories punctuate the work. It's too long ago to remember exact conversations, but some went like this:

"My Dad and his friend were walking toward Pechanga," my Uncle Peanut says. "It was hot and they had come a long way. A car slowed down. 'You guys tired of walking?' said the passenger. 'Heck, yes,' my Dad said. 'Well try running then,' the man said laughing. The car spun off. Oh, my Dad was mad."

Stories drop from our mouths the way seeds drop into sacks. Woven like orange widows hair on buckwheat, the stories enfold us, comfort us, make us laugh. Our lives are retold the way beans are refried.

"Ol Rat's Ass came home drunk the other night," Cool City says.

"That's news?" my uncle asks.

"He was hungry. But the fridge was empty. So he fried the goldfish. Caught his kids' goldfish from the fishbowl and fried them in a pan. Ain't that sumpthin'?"

Indian life refried.

His Name Still A Mystery, He Was No Chicken

Sure, he drank too much.

If he could have done any better at sobriety, he would have.

But Verle "Chicken" Rodriguez found escape in the bottle, a numbness, a haven from what haunted him. He found solace in wine, the way a sinner finds deliverance in the confessional. So, yes, he drank too much.

But he wasn't just a drunken Indian. He was more than Thunderbird fumes. More than bloodshot eyes that swam like heartbreak in tomato soup. More than morning shakes and wine-knotted insides.

I don't know his full history. He's gone. Most of his blood siblings are gone. There's few left to ask. The truth is buried with him in the Pala Indian Reservation graveyard.

Hearsay passes for biography now. And most of what I know, comes from what I've heard. But I knew Chicken.

And I drank with him on occasion and considered him a friend. I write about him because I think his life counted.

They say World War II changed him. That he returned a different man. He never talked about his war experiences. But if you looked, you could see the imprint, the indelible, telltale mark of ordeal that wouldn't let go.

It's not like he didn't try. Chicken had binges of sobriety. He'd wear clean T-shirts and freshly laundered khaki pants. He'd tie his black oxfords and shave close, leaving only a close-trimmed mustache. He'd slick back his hair, and smile with a crooked tilt.

And he was a handsome man. His boxer's nose a bit bent from heavy blows, his eyebrows nicked with scars. He walked with slightly rounded shoulders, like a man accustomed to fighting from a crouch.

When sober, Chicken didn't talk much. He shunned rez society, evaded the shaded circle of chairs where the men sat passing the jug and spouting false bravado.

Instead, Chicken hoed in his yard. He hoed around his rose bushes, blading the ground, cutting any weed that dared encroach his space. He liked flowers, especially roses, and took pride in them. And he hoed around his chili plants. And if you asked him, he'd give you a handful of yellow chilies.

I'd take them home to my grandmother and we'd munch them at lunch, crunching into the chili then biting into fresh tortillas rolled with avocado, onion, lime, salt and pepper.

For weeks, he'd do so well, you'd start think this was the one, this time he'd stay sober. But then you'd see him on an orange crate in Fernando's yard, his index finger pressing the corner of his mouth, his hair disheveled, his face flushed, his eyes a glassy mask.

From left field, no matter what anybody else was saying, he'd bellow: "Well, what about me? I want to get married. Why can't I have a woman?"

Then he realized he knew the answer to his own question. And he'd laugh to himself, press his finger to the corner of his mouth and sing a few lines from "Deep in the Heart of Texas."

I don't know why people called him Chicken. He was far from chicken.

In the circle of drinkers at Fernando's there was a big man named Victor Smith.

A southpaw, Victor would say, "My right will cut you, but my left will knock you out." He'd ball his hands into fists: "These hands are dynamite."

Then from another country Chicken would say, "Ah, balls."

And things would escalate from there.

By this time, both Victor and Chicken were in their 50s, but what the two men lacked in youth, they made up for in swagger. Soon they'd be swinging.

It could happen anywhere. At a ballgame. At a dance. In Fernando's yard. The two fought like sparring partners. Sometimes Vic would win. Sometimes Chicken. I think it depended on who had more wine.

But Chicken was never chicken. Foolhardy maybe. But never chicken.

Twice, at fiestas, I saw Chicken reach into a fire, pluck out a coal, pop it into his mouth and chew it until it was out.

It must have blistered his tongue. But like Indian fire-eaters of old, he did it. That's what amazed me. He did it. Dang, I thought.

Closing A Portal To Past; Opening One To Promise

Metal against metal, like a blacksmith hammering a horseshoe, a pile driver clangs on the Pala Indian Reservation.

From morning till night, weighted machinery bangs pylons into the sand of the San Luis Rey River bottom.

The clanging has become the metronome of our lives, measuring the moments until we become "Casino Indians."

Work has begun on the gaming facility that many dream will lift us to a new prosperity.

Day by day, the casino takes shape on what used to be Acorn Park, the old campgrounds. At least a dozen old oak trees were yanked out to make way for the casino. A snarl of sawed limbs tangled on a bare spot of earth is all that remains. Work crews will cut trees into cordwood and distribute it to elders.

We drove by the other day, and my son noticed all the construction. "It's all going to change, Dad," Bear said. "It's never going to be the same, is it?"

"Not likely," I replied.

Bear turned wistful about the campground, about the fiesta nights there, sitting around fires watching peon games until early morning.

He thinks of the casino as an interloper, an interruption to a lifestyle he's grown up in. But then Bear has never known real poverty the way some Pala Indians have known poverty. Which is why I've tried to remain neutral about the casino.

People often ask me about Indian casinos.

As I've written before, I'm not a fan of casinos. I rarely go into them, except to watch boxing or hear some music, or to graze on cheap steak and eggs. I don't gamble much. In a casino, I play a little slow death (keno), drink a few free cocktails and people-watch.

Oh, I'll sit down to a little poker with the boys, and I don't mind a $2 bet here and there on the horses. But I simply hate to lose. The pain of losing exceeds the joy of winning.

Bottom line, I wish Indians could find a more dignified way of achieving prosperity. I hate to think of the addicted gamblers who gamble away their happiness, ruin their families, lose not only their lives but their sense of self-worth. So I challenge Indian casinos to spot problem gamblers and offer help in the way of counseling.

Yes, gaming has downsides, but for now, Indians view gaming as a portal to the American dream. And I think it's time Indians got a seat at the banquet table. So I back the Indian's right to sovereignty and self-determination and the choice to pursue gaming as a livelihood.

Pala Indians have been poor for a long time, but they've also been able to turn hardship into a laughing matter.

For instance, an Indian couple stops at the grocery store.

"What are we stopping here for?" the man asks.

"I need to pick up some Indian steak," the woman replies.

The man nods his head, leans back, and listens to the game on the radio.

The woman heads not for the meats, but for the deli counter. Oscar Mayer? No, the house brand is cheaper. She grabs a couple of packs of bologna.

On the rez, Indian steak means bologna. Unable to afford T-bone or porterhouse, we bought bologna. We ate it for breakfast. Ever have fried balogna and powdered eggs? For lunch, on tortillas with mayo and mustard. For dinner, in thick sandwiches on Wonder Bread with commodity cheese.

In the not too bygone days, an Indian car was something to behold. Used to be, you could even go into an Indian shop and buy an "Indian Car" bumper sticker.

An Indian car was most properly a long, low, dented-up gas hog with a straightened clothes hanger for a radio antenna. No self-respecting Indian car had all of its hubcaps. Seat covers might be an olive-drab Army blanket so seat springs didn't poke you in the rear. Hang a couple of feathers from the rearview mirror and pour in some Ray Lube oil so it didn't smoke too much and you had a prize Indian car fit for the powwow highway.

Maybe, once the casino arrives, we can drive all the Indian cars to the junkyard where they belong.

From Tiny Acorns, Mighty Thoughts Grow

With the arrival of autumn, the acorns ripen in the hills, falling like heaven's manna onto brittle oak leaves that crackle with the comedown.

In the days before drive-through Taco Bells and curly fries and corn dogs at AM/PM, Indians here relied on acorns.

In the fall, when acorns heavy with nutrients dropped, the people bent at the waist and plucked them from the ground, dropping them into tightly woven carrying baskets.

They then stored the acorns in big, twig-woven granaries and when the harvest was good, the acorns would last clear round to the next harvest. I'm sure it was some kid's job to run to granary and fetch a basketful of acorns for his mother who would grind the meats into flour.

Take a walk in woodsy areas of the county and you'll often encounter big slabs of granite pocked by milling depressions formed by women pounding and grinding acorn meats into a fine flour with a stone pestle.

I believe, Indian people had a vastly different perspective of time in those days. Women would sit for hours in the sun, grinding acorns while singing songs. And if Indian women of long ago were anything like Indian women of today, they must have talked — gossiped if you will — about the village goings-on as they worked.

Or when they didn't talk, and when the song rhythms and the work rhythms synchronized, I imagine the work could mesmerize, providing hypnotic conduits to another reality.

Back then there was no room for impatience. Now, Indians fidget and grouse when the next line at supermarket counter moves faster than the one we're in.

We roll our eyes. We think: More dirty dealings of an impertinent world, always sticking us in the slowest line. And we pout at the unfairness.

Once Indian people walked miles to sit around evening fires for conversation with other Indian people. But now even rotary dial is too slow for us, so we touchtone dial and add speed dial to that. Then we grumble when the other end doesn't pick up immediately.

Or we gnash our teeth when the computer modem takes its sweet time downloading from the Net. We feel put upon. Once Indians wandered mountain trails searching for enlightenment. Now our life is a quest for a faster modem.

I've never taken the time to make weewish, the acorn mush that once anchored the Indian diet. My brother did once, but it was gritty and unappetizing, clearly the product of a rookie.

Instead, I buy weewish from one the handful of people who still make it, placing an order in time for Thanksgiving or Christmas dinner. And it comes in an aluminum foil pan like a Sarah Lee cake.

Gone are the stone-ground days. Now people use blenders or food processors — real time savers. And the mush is cooked stove top, poured into foil pans and then frozen for safekeeping.

Many Indians, especially kids, have lost the taste for weewish. Raised on Hostess Twinkies and Pepsi, weewish is much too bland to excite the palate of the young.

But many elders still enjoy weewish, even if it is only served ceremoniously at special dinners. It makes a nice holiday gift.

I've been to funerals on the Barona Indian Reservation where they served weewish. Only these Kumeyaay Indians call it shawee. It's no different though.

I wish I could describe what it tastes. I wish I could say it tastes like plain Cream of Wheat or sugarless rice pudding or corn meal mush. But it's unique, a taste unto itself and I can't compare it to anything.

Those who don't like it, say it tastes earthy, almost like dirt. But those who do like it, say it tastes of home, of dinner at grandmother's house, of their youth.

Most Indians like it with beans and salsa. That's the way I prefer it, a forkful saturated with bean juice and hot serrano-chili salsa. Or rolled into a bit of tortilla with some hot beef stew.

And, to me, it tastes of time compressed, of women singing on a granite outcropping, of cooking fires, of wildness.

Bench Served As Perfect Place To Talk And Sing

Countless Levis and khaki rubbings from the backsides of world-watchers rounded the edges of the Old Man's Bench.

In its prime, the bench had a patina of time, darkened by weather and spilled wine. Kids with penknives carved nicknames into the wood. Old men, whiling away the hours, scratched the wood with fingernails yellowed by hand-rolled Bull Durham and Prince Albert cigarettes.

Really, the Old Man's Bench, which everybody called it, was just a couple of boards nailed to span two eucalyptus trees, no scrolled iron work, no fancy handiwork. Just scrap lumber nailed across trees.

If you look real close, you can still see bench shards embedded in the gnarled trees. But the bench's time is gone. Just as time has expired for most of the men who sat on it. Gone.

But they had their lives. They had their flow of moments, their experiences that became the substance of their talk.

The bench was at the crossroads of the Pala Indian Reservation, just down from the mission and across the street from the Pala Store.

It seemed the world's oldest bull session, a daily gathering place for graybeards to sit and check pocket watches that measured how time moseyed.

My grandfather, Paul Magee, had a pocket watch tied to a belt loop with a leather thong in the watch-pocket of his Levis. When he'd see me passing he'd pull the watch out and check the time.

"Better get home, boy, about time for your lunch," he'd say.

He wasn't fooling me. I knew he sent me away so he could drink from a half-gallon of port wine unmolested by a my prying eyes.

I'm not sure if anybody knows who first happened upon the idea to nail up the bench.

Before the bench existed, men sat on a concrete ledge that jutted from the foundation of the mission rock wall.

But then traffic along Pala Mission Road picked up, and a blind spot made crossing the road to the store risky, so the men moved to the bench sometime in the 1940s I'd guess.

And they'd gather in the pungent eucalyptus shade, to talk, to laugh, to sing, to recount whatever they deemed memorable.

Horsemen like Remijio Lugo and Joe Nejo would tie up their mounts in the pepper-tree shade behind the store, then amble to the eucalyptus tree shade to see what was doing with friends like Jack **Johnson,** Steve Lugo, Sam Barker, Salvario Chavez, the Blacktooth brothers and numerous others.

Many of the old timers would stop in for a few minutes of gab, just enough to catch up on the latest — who was caught sleeping with who, why so and so had a black eye, did somebody's dog get shot for chasing cattle? Curiosity sated, they'd go back to splitting wood or hoeing gardens or plucking chickens or whatever.

Some, would spend all day at the bench. Especially, if a jug of wine materialized. Wine enlivened the conversation, but also made things unpredictable.

A whittled-stick handle shoved into an evaporated milk can with several pebbles inside would suffice as a rattle. And the men would sing old songs, songs that their fathers and grandfathers sang. And you could walk by the store and hear the ancient rhythms accent the afternoon and hear the gravely voices trill in unison.

All of life unfolded at the bench. Sometimes, when the wine overpowered sensibilities, men would succumb to a sense of the forlorn. And tears would flow, tears of remorse for a thing done or not done, tears of grief for a departed loved one, tears of self-recrimination for a wasted life, tears of frustration for all the hard work without much pay of Indian life.

The bench is gone now. The eucalyptus trees grew and bowed the bench until it split and had to be cut out. And most of the men are gone too. But at that corner, their spirits continue.

Stand there and listen to the Pacific breezes rattle the eucalyptus leaves and you can year rattles and songs and talk and wails of the old men.

They had their time. We have ours.

Gordon Johnson

Candlelight Flickers To Honor The Dead

It's a black-and-white tradition, white moonlight slanting across black granite gravestones, with yellow candlelight the only interruption to shades of gray.

All Soul's Day or Day of the Dead or Dia de los Muertos or as many Indians simply call it — Candlelighting — happens tonight.

And for as long as anyone can remember, on this night Indian people of Southern California honor the dead by lighting candles at cemeteries.

Pala reservation has two cemeteries. The smaller cemetery, nearly 200 years old, is located next to the mission, the other larger cemetery, only about 100 years old, is a couple of blocks up the road.

For Candlelighting, I go to the larger cemetery, where my grandparents and other relatives are buried.

Big pepper trees, with branches tangled like a sleeping girl's hair, spice the air. Dried peppercorns litter the graves like spilt BBs. Small peppery leaves flutter like moth wings in the Pacific breeze.

The graves march in orderly rows, not in chronological order of death, but in family groups: Ortega, Owlingwish, Nolasquez, Diaz, Chutnicutt, Trujillo and so on.

Loved-ones place items of meaning on graves. Statues of the Virgin Mary. Porcelain doves on the wing. Concrete fish. Gift-shop vases with plastic ferns. Small American flags for military men. A Notre Dame cap for a diehard Irish fan. One young boy's grave sports a maple syrup bottle. A fondness for pancakes perhaps?

At quiet graves, moss creeps along crosses of wood and concrete. Many crosses mark unnamed graves, graves that have been there so long, no one remembers who lies beneath the sod.

But on the Day of the Dead, even forgotten graves get candles of recognition. At Candlelighting, candles by the thousands flicker heavenward, until the night sky glows.

This year, King Freeman, owner of the Pala store, ordered 6,000 candles. But the people asked for more. He's placed another order, now he hopes the extras arrive in time.

The graveyard's centerpiece is a concrete cross atop a river-rock base. In an unstudied hand, somebody scratched "May they rest in peace," in the cross's wet cement. Now the message invokes permanence.

After years of serving as a convenient candle spot, candle smoke has blackened the river rocks and rivulets of hardened wax drip like milky tears.

Tonight, Pala people will cover up sadness with greetings and soft jokes. The occasion is never too solemn, never too grave. Except at graves of the freshly dead, where the wounds of grief haven't had time to heal.

Tonight, the people gather. Tonight an old woman in a head scarf and a woolen coat will wander the graveyard and kneel to light candles for those she has outlived.

And an old man, in a Levi jacket and work boots, might pour a beer on the grave of an old drinking buddy.

And the dead will be remembered. For how are they to achieve any measure of immortality if we don't remember?

My grandmother habitually made a big deal of Candlelighting. She ordered her candles well in advance.

She made sure kitchen matches filled her sweater pockets.

At the first darkening of the day, with the sun just dipping to the West, she'd light out in her tennis-shoed gait toward the cemetery, her box of candles under her arm.

And she'd wander the rows of graves and mentally reconstruct the faces that once peopled her life. The birthday parties, the weddings, the ballgames, the baby showers, the funerals, the events made special by the people who now serve as resting places for artificial flowers.

All along the way, she'd stop to light candles and pray.

After my grandfather died in 1987, she'd stand at his grave for a long time, candlelight reflected in her tears, and silently scold him for leaving her alone.

Tonight the graveyard is alive with people who sit in lawn chairs or stand with arms folded and visit with the dead.

And as moonlight congregates with candlelight on this black-and-white night, immortality is served.

Aunt Martha's Songs Of Life

A steamer trunk of leather straps and sun-worn planks squats out of place on her living room floor.

A lifetime of photos and sacramental certificates fill the trunk in striated layers, counting backwards through the years like an archaeologist's excavation.

The old photos depict a life lived in black and white. In one photo, my Aunt Martha, skinny as a noodle, stands in front of the slat house with her brothers and sisters: Vivian, Delfreda, Alvino, Peter. Only her brother Florian was missing.

Of her siblings, Aunt Martha wasn't the youngest, but she was the last. In the photo she looked so fresh, so immune to old age. But she wasn't. My Aunt Martha died last week at age 81. And her death marks an end.

With her death, the family Bible closed. A nuclear family fissioned. The Trujillos born of Peter and Espranza became past tense.

You see, she was my grandmother's little sister. The gap-toothed one my grandmother teased, "Yeah, well, you weren't even born with us. Momma found you down at the river."

In the old days, the San Luis Rey River seemed a living presence. As a young girl, Aunt Martha bathed in shallow river pools, lathering with a soap plant they called nikish, or bitter balls.

On laundry days, they kneeled on the banks, sand biting into their knees, to scrub clothes on the rocks, using a soap home-rendered from pork fat and lye.

121

And the girls sang at the river, a funny Cupeno frog song, hopping until they fell over from laughter.

When she was young, feet bare, her dress stitched from flour sacks, Aunt Martha helped pick spinach in her father's field across the river. She cleaned pinto beans, yanked strings from string beans, husked white corn, carried wood for the wood stove. She milked the cow, carrying fresh-squeezed milk to her mother. Of her mother, Aunt Martha once told me, "Mamma was always comical, but she didn't mean to be."

And she told the story about how her mother, a very religious woman, came home from church one day holding back tears.

"Momma, what's the matter?" Aunt Martha asked.

"Oh, I'm so disappointed," her mother said. "The priest said a bad word in church today ... He said ass."

Of course, he was talking about Mary riding a donkey, but in Espranza's missionized mind, the priest had blasphemed in church. Aunt Martha got a kick out of that. And it became a defining memory.

Things changed when Aunt Martha was about 8. Her father died. And Aunt Martha was sent to St. Boniface School in Banning. Away from family, she felt abandoned. At home life was hard, but at least there was love. At St. Boniface, she was forced to sing church hymns with her knees pressed into the cold wood of church pews.

When at home, Aunt Martha and her sisters sang in the shade of an apricot tree that grew by the bedroom window.

Sometimes they sang a Cupeno song about a mother who finds her children chased by a bear onto a rock. And then, by way of mother's magic, the children fly from the rocks to safety.

And it was a mother's magic that kept Aunt Martha's two sons, Robert Banks and Stanley McGarr, alive. Both sons lived in wildness. Both sons have at times been stranded on the rocks. Both are still alive, in part anyway, because of mother's magic.

Johnny "Chucie" Chutnicut, my Aunt's mate of more than 40 years, rummages through the trunk, looking for a deer-toe rattle he wants to bury with Aunt Martha. The rattle belonged to her step-father, a man of power everyone called Uncle Jack.

The room, the whole empty house, echoes with her absence. "We were so simple together, that's the thing," he says, awash in memories. "We were never apart."

And he'll never hear, and I'll never hear, her voice behind us, singing the peon songs, singing us on — win or lose — to play a worthy game.

She sang of Indian life in songs that transform a cruel world to one of mystery.

She and the songs will be missed.

What I Wouldn't Give For Just One Cigarette

I'm sitting at this cussed computer Friday afternoon, trying to come up with a column, and all I can think of is how badly I want a Camel.

My lungs scream to be filled with smoke, my insides churn with pent up anxiety, I'm wound up like a death row inmate facing a firing squad.

And then I think, even the blindfolded inmate gets a cigarette before eating bullets. Me, I only have day after gut-ripping day of a smoke-free life to look forward to.

Yes, I've quit - again. But the fates seem to be conspiring to suck me back into the grasp of demon weed.

First thing this morning, my 6-year-old son Bear shook me awake with a gasp and said: "Dad, you know our dog Gypsy was bumped by a car just now. Her insides are squished all over the road."

Poor Bear had run up from the school bus stop to tell me one of our little dachshunds, the prettier of the two, was now a road kill.

The doxies habitually followed the kids in the morning to the bus stop. This time one didn't return.

My first reaction after hearing the news was to reach for the pack of cigarettes on the night stand to quell the sick feeling that came over me. I really liked that dog.

But since I quit smoking, there were no smokes to be had. So I steeled myself for the unpleasantness ahead - picking up and burying the dog - without a cigarette.

No need for gory details here. Let's just say that throwing dirt over my flattened jogging partner was no fun.

To help lift my mood, I decided to grab a cup of tea with my old buddy Jean Jackson.

"One of my little dogs got bumped this morning," I told him, as I sipped the hot brew.

"Aw, that's a shame," he said. As a man who has had dogs all his life, he knew exactly how I felt.

The dog mourning was soon interrupted as a hard-drinking woman named Joy, who hails from Lake Elsinore but has been staying in Pala, knocked on the screen door.

"Morning," she said in a whiskey-and-cigarette voice that crackled like dried leaves.

As soon as she sat down, she pulled out a crumpled pack of generic cigarettes and lit one up.

The room soon filled with acrid smoke and chatter from her about Lake Elsinore: morning happy hour at The Wreck, a Christmas card from city Councilwoman Tere Cherveny with a ten-spot in it, pigeon hunting at city Councilman Fred Dominguez's barber shop.

As she rambled, she chained smoked, and it was all I could do to keep from bumming one from her.

When I couldn't stand watching her puff away any longer, I left for home to eat breakfast.

Normally, I read the morning newspaper with my Raisin Bran, but for some reason, I didn't get a newspaper, so I plucked "The Singapore Wink" by Ross Thomas from my bookshelves.

I have read the book several times, and I was just reading it because I always read something during breakfast. I opened it to a random page near the middle.

Right off the bat, Mark and Carla, the protagonists, were sitting in a Singapore bar, drinking cocktails and smoking cigarettes.

Mark glances at the ashtray and counts four butts that Carla has smoked in the last hour.

"You sure smoke a lot," he comments.

"I know," she says, lighting another.

Is there no getting away from it, I ask myself?

I read on. Soon Mark is sitting in the office of Singapore's chief of secret police. The Chinese policeman is dressed as a businessman, in gray slacks, crisp white shirt and conservative tie.

With little ceremony, he pours out tea from a ceramic pot and offers Mark a Lucky Strike.

Mark accepts one and fires it up. The policeman lights one as well, inhaling deeply, with great satisfaction.

"American cigarettes are one of my vices," he says.

Yeah, mine too, I thought.

Well, it's rugged, but I'm still hanging in there. God, I wish I had never started smoking.

Take my word for it: Don't light up.

Standing Tall In The Midst Of Hard Times

Most of the leaves on our old elderberry trees dropped months ago, leaving a determined few still clutching to barren branches.

Through the blistering Santa Ana winds and the near-freezing nights, these leaves prevail. The kicked soccer ball barreling through the branches hasn't knocked them off. Neither has Nushe our Siamese cat, chasing after song birds, nor mountain pigeons flitting from branch to branch in search of ripe elderberries.

Other leaves on the same tree let go at the first sign of trouble, falling effortlessly to the ground, giving themselves up to mulch with nary a whimper. But these remaining leaves, these stalwart ones, are made of sterner stuff. They won't say die.

Sometimes I feel like one of those hangers-on, one of those stragglers clinging for dear life to a hope that's bound to disappoint.

Sunday morning, I clambered out of bed, slipped into some sweats and tennis shoes, and headed out the door for a slow jog.

The sun had topped the piney mountain ridges to the east, throwing a crisp, yellow light across the distant brushy hills and sandy washes of the Pala Indian Reservation. And Gypsy, our ankle-high dachshund, eager for the morning run, bounced against my legs, her little tail whipping up a joyous beat. It was a grand morning. I stretched a little as I walked down the driveway, trying to loosen the sleep-knotted muscles in my back and legs. At the bottom of the driveway, I spotted the Sunday paper, all rolled up in a plastic bag.

An incurable news junkie, I picked it up and scanned the front page before lighting out on my run. It was a big mistake.

My heart sank, my gut tightened up. Saturday evening; they found the 12-year-old Petaluma girl who was abducted at knifepoint from her home. Polly Klaas' body was located in a wooded thicket near Highway 101 about 30 miles north of Petaluma.

Hurriedly, I rolled up the newspaper and stuck it back into its plastic bag, hoping I could put the death of that innocent girl out of mind. But it was too late.

Sometimes I can run through my troubles, the thud of my feet on the dirt road seemingly pounding the worries out of me. But this morning, my running only churned up more bad thoughts, so I slowed to a walk.

As I passed the big sycamore tree, the one playing host to the mistletoe on its branches, I remembered the home videos of Polly seen on television news. So lithe and lively, with an infectious smile, she mugged for the video camera.

Was it her dad who kept her centered in the viewfinder as she danced on the front lawn?

I imagined the anguish of her parents, the horrible hole in their hearts, a vacuum sucking the life right out of them.

Then I got a bad case of the "what ifs," and did the whole "what if it were my daughter?" routine.

Images of my 13-year-old daughter's birth came to mind, her first birthday party, holding her hands as she learned to walk, her smile as she smeared chocolate pudding on her face, the Father/Daughter Valentine's Dance and all the rest.

That made me feel even worse. What an awful thing grief is, what despair it unleashes, what emotional pathos it wreaks.

How does one cope?

I walked along, and gave that some thought. About this time I came across the carcass of a road runner on the side of the trail. Freshly dead, the ants and other insects hadn't yet feasted. It's head rested in the sand, it's dead black eye stared back up at me.

It was that cold, empty stare that lifted me out of my funk. Life seemed to regain purpose and order. Remain strong, I told myself, like the last of the elderberry leaves. The struggle is the thing. Both curse and blessing.

One look at the road runner's lifeless eye, and I knew that life, in all its travail, is better than the alternative.

Self Esteem Has Got Our House By The Throat

When Adam and Eve fell from grace, God not only banished them forever from the Garden of Eden, but for added punishment, he visited them with an unholy plague - teen-agers.

Teen-agers. God bless `em. Right now, I'm blessed with two teens in the house: Missy, 13, and Tyra, who will be 17 on Thursday. (Happy Birthday, pumkin').

Always in the back of my mind, I wonder if I'm doing right by them. There are so many prevailing theories, everything from tough love to total leniency, that it's hard to know what's right.

As a teen of the 60s, I picked up a few child-rearing techniques from the social visionaries of the time. They saw our generation as the first to cut through the phony double standards of a plastic society, to raise our love children in a new spirit of freedom.

All across the country, kids named Rainbow and Aurora and Sky ran around the house buck naked, peeing wherever they wanted, including on Santana, the black lab with the red bandana for a collar.

These kids breakfasted on granola, lunched on brown rice and dined on lentil soup. They crafted God's eyes with yarn and Popsicle sticks instead of watching TV. They knew all the words to "Stairway to Heaven" before they could walk.

Dad wore Birkenstocks, not wingtips, and smoked good buds in his pipe instead of Prince Albert. And mom, who just started shaving her legs and armpits a few years ago, still smells of baker's yeast and stone-ground whole wheat.

But I guess, I was too much from the old school to buy into the hippie child-rearing bit.

My kids wore Pampers, dad gummit. I did worry over the plastic or cloth dilemma for a time, but much of our early child rearing was done when we didn't own a washing machine. So we bought Pampers, or Huggies, or Luvs or whatever was on sale.

And my kids didn't eat like Buddhist monks, either. They had eggs and bacon and white-bread toast. They had every kind of sugar-coated cereal they ever saw advertised on TV. They listened to country music and the blues and Motown. To this day I don't think my kids have even heard Led Zeppelin's "Stairway to Heaven." If they did, they didn't hear it from me.

And they weren't coddled. Why, when they acted up, I yelled at them. When they really acted up, I whacked them and sent them to their rooms.

Heck, there were plenty of times my dad welted my backside with a hand-carved oak paddle to set me on the straight and narrow. So I figured my kids would survive a swat to the rump now and then without permanent damage to their self-esteem.

Self-esteem. There's a concept that's blackened my doorstep.

"Don't yell at your kids, it might bruise their self-esteem," the experts say. "Whatever you do, don't spank your kids, their self-esteem might come totally unhinged," they say.

Back in my day, we never had any self-esteem. If you went around saying, "I like myself, I like myself," people would think you were conceited big-time.

Over the years, I've been so careful of my kids self-esteem, now I think they have too much of the stuff. They're so full of it, they think of themselves as the axis around which the cosmos rotates.

If you doubt me, just listen in:

"Tyra would you please do the dishes?"

"Ohhhhhh, dad," she says exasperated. "I haven't got time. Debbie's coming by any minute to pick me up for the show. By the way, can I have $10 to get in."

In a parental daze, I hand her the money. A horn honks, and she's out the door.

"Missy, will you please do the dishes?"

"Guuuuuuyyyy, dad," she whines. "It's not my turn. I did them last time."

I plead: "Can't you please do them, and I'll make Tyra do `em twice in a row."

Begins the tirade: "Oh, why did I have to be born in this house? Why couldn't I have parents with a dishwasher? Better yet, with a maid? Why do I have to do everything ...?"

I often wonder if a little more oat bran in their early upbringing would have made a difference?

Back When The Fourth Had A Bigger Bang

I know it's for their own good, but I can't help thinking that kids today get the short end of the punk when it comes to Fourth of July fun.

Oh sure, we treat our kids to the latest in pyrotechnics these days, with cannons pounding fireworks skyward while folks sit on blankets, oohing and aahing at the razzle-dazzle in the firmament.

But for all their brilliance, the $20,000 extravaganzas can't hold a candle to the simple thrill of a nickel sparkler in a 5-year-old's hand.

Dangerous, yes, but I miss the days when fireworks were legal.

The magic for me would start with the first sighting of a roadside fireworks stand.

"RED DEVIL FIREWORKS SOLD HERE - CHEAP," the hand-painted signs would scream. We'd pedal our bikes past the makeshift stands to feast on the wonder of it all - the Whistling Petes, the Volcanoes, the huge Roman candles beckoning with the promise of sky-high fanfare.

Usually, there were package deals available, from the small, sissy $5 box to the Super-Duper Special with 110 pieces for the low, low price of $35.

Even as a kid, I knew that if you held out, you might get a better deal if on the last day the vendor ran scared and dropped his prices.

Never eager to throw away money, especially on stuff that was going up in smoke anyway, my dad usually waited till the bitter end to buy, hoping the $35 pack had been slashed to $25, or better yet, $20.

Mom, however, would buy the $35 pack and a dozen or so big Roman candles right off the bat, keep them hidden, and then spring them on everybody - including Dad - toward the end.

When it came to fireworks, Mom was a class act.

Along with the sparkle, there was the taste of Fourth of July - fresh potato salad with olives, pickles and paprika mounded next to a flotilla of spicy chili beans, along with half a grilled chicken, the skin crispy with charred sauce, the white meat juicy and smoky from the fire.

Wash it down with lemonade and finish with a big hunk of cold watermelon.

"I can spit the seeds further than you," a cousin would say, and each bite would be punctuated with a "ptuey."

"Mine went farther."

"You're nuts, mine did."

And so it went, until the last of the watermelon juice and chicken grease was wiped on your shirt and the real fun began.

Somebody, an older cousin or friend, would always come by with firecrackers for sale.

"Mom, can I have a dollar?" And good ol' Mom would reach into her purse.

The firecrackers came two rows to a pack, with individual fuses laced to a big fuse. If you were crazy, you could fire up the whole pack by putting a match to the main fuse, but I figured there was more fun to be had lighting them one at a time.

In a way, firecrackers were part of a kid's foray into science.

Take a coffee can, put about four inches of water in the bottom, take a small fruit can, empty out the fruit (in the trash if you had to), and punch a hole in its top big enough for a firecracker. Take the open end of the fruit can, set it into the water of the coffee can, insert the firecracker into the hole at the top, and light the fuse.

"Kerpow!" With the right amount of water, the fruit can would shoot a good 25 feet or so into the air.

It was also fun to see how high an unsuspecting girl in a ponytail and bobby socks would jump when a firecracker blasted off behind her.

And when it got dark enough, sparklers were great fun too.

You could stand there and pretend you were the Statue of Liberty. You could have sword fights. You could make designs in the air, like big hearts for the pretty little girl from down the road, the same one you scared with a firecracker earlier.

Finally, when the last of the sparklers was gone, the kids would sit back and let the adults light the big ones.

Volcanoes erupted, Petes whistled, and at least one of the big, expensive Roman candles would be a dud.

"Ohhhhh," everyone would say. And somehow, even the duds were fun.

A Little Perspective

On Sunday, Santa Ana winds swooped down on us in scorching gusts that dried our skin and frayed our nerves.

In the house, our tired air conditioner worked overtime, and every ceiling fan and table fan we could muster was switched to high, but still we simmered like a beef stew.

With the curtains drawn, and the shades down, the kids huddled around the TV in the dim living room, bickering over what to watch.

"I want to watch cartoons," Bear, 7, whined.

"I got dibs, let's turn it to Save the Bell," Missy, 14, countered.

"I'm the oldest, and I want to watch a movie," Tyra, 17, demanded.

Only Brandon, 12, didn't raise Cain. Weary of the ruckus, he hoofed it out the door to hang out with friends.

On and on it went - the teasing, the arguing, the name calling - a typical Sunday in the Johnson house.

They sprawled like wilted cabbages on the couches and on the floor, with only a foot here and a hand there wiggling - too hot to move, too bored to lie still.

Then without warning, the power went out. The air conditioner stopped chugging. The fans died. The TV went dark. The kids went berserk.

I knew it wouldn't take long. And it didn't.

"It's boring, dad, let's go to the show," Bear said.

"Dad, let's go to the Rincon softball games," Tyra said.

"Dad, can we at least take the truck and go buy a pop or something?" asked Missy.

Non-stop harangue. They pulled out every ploy in the book to get me to rescue them from their malaise.

"Is this all I am to them? Cruise director for their rudderless ship? Making sure they're entertained while their ship steams in circles?" I thought to myself.

"Do something constructive," I yelled. "Read a book. Get a head start on a school project. Clean your rooms. Do something worthwhile with your time. Just leave me alone."

But pretty soon, the electricity returned, and they resumed lounging, moving only now and then to fight over the remote control.

I don't mind saying, I was pretty fed up with them. "Worthless kids," I muttered.

But when I got to work Monday morning, my sentiments changed.

"Two teens die, four hurt in accident," the headline read.

Three Temecula Valley High School football players and their girlfriends rolled off a Highway 101 embankment Saturday morning near Santa Maria.

Samuel Couch, 16, and Autumn Harkey, 15, didn't make it. Ryan Nau and Lyle Thomas Knode, both 16, were critically injured. Kylie Mullins, 15, and Heidi Groff, 16, were treated and released.

It was supposed to be a fun trip. An early-morning excursion full of laughs to visit Couch's older sister, Rachel, who attends college in San Luis Obispo.

But something went wrong.

I stared at Autumn's photo in the newspaper. Shiny dark hair, Pepsodent smile, freckles sprinkled across her cheeks, eyes that lit up with her smile.

My God, she could have passed as a sister to my daughters.

And Sam Couch, with his wry football squint, tight-lipped grin, and that confident look that says, "Hey, I can dance"; well, in four years, my son, Brandon, could have the same look.

It could have been my kids. It could have been your kids. But this time it was Autumn Harkey and Sam Couch.

My heart goes out to the parents. I know as a parent what it must feel like. There's no greater loss than the loss of a child, and I pray the Creator gives them strength to bear up under the pain.

But as parents, what are we to do? We can't cage our teens up. We can't deny them life's experiences. And even when we try, it doesn't always work out. Autumn didn't have her parents' permission to go. She went on her own.

No, I just don't have any answers.

But here's my plan. I'm going to do a better job of showing my children I love them. I'm going to embrace them more, tell them I love them more often, and talk to them more as people, instead of dictator to serf.

And the next time my kids ask to do something with me, dang it, I'm going to do it.

Meanwhile, kids, please take care.

Contemplating The Clouds And The Chowder

A three-quarter moon, pale as whale bone, played peekaboo behind clouds that stretched across the night sky like Rorschach ink blots.

A bull sea lion, lolling on flat support beams beneath the Santa Cruz pier, barked irascibly at the others sprawled nearby as if to say, "Shut up, I'm trying to sleep." His rebukes, however, only provoked more barking from the herd. No rest for the weary, I guess.

Ocean breezes, lush with the scent of salt and fish, blew cold enough to redden your nose and make you glad you had a sweater. But they were refreshing winds, brisk with autumn, that begged to be inhaled deep into the lungs.

A lifetime ago, while at the University of California, Santa Cruz, I used to ride my 10-speed down to this pier to sit on a bench and read Camus as the sun went down. When the action got good, I'd abandon my book to watch a fisherman reel in a perch or a sand shark or maybe some seaweed. And when the fishing boats docked, I liked to watch the deck hands filet the catch, cutting swift and sure with thin-bladed knives. There I'd sit, reading and watching, until it got too dark to see.

For dinner, I'd step into a little restaurant near the end of the pier called Stagnaro's for a bowl of clam chowder, some French bread and a beer.

I've always liked the place. It had the look and feel of the cafe in Alfred Hitchcock's film, "The Birds," and any minute I expected Tippi Hedren to saunter in. I'd take a small booth near the window and slurp my chowder as sailboats, tethered to floats, bobbed in the swell and seagulls perched one-legged on pier railings.

We were in Santa Cruz for an old high school buddy's wedding, but when in the area, my wife, Nadine, and I always try to stop in at Stagnaro's for a bite. It's kind of a tradition with us.

Unfortunately, all things change. It must be a compulsion with folks not to leave well enough alone. In 1988, work crews attacked the place in a sad attempt to make it bigger and better. They knocked down the walls, and added glitz, nearly obliterating the 1940s charm.

But garish cosmetics aside, it's still a swell restaurant, and even with the brass fixtures and hanging ferns, they couldn't do anything to sour the view.

So we still come back.

A waifish woman in white blouse baggier than a night shirt showed us to our booth and handed menus around.

Above us, the words "seafood cocktails" glowed in pink neon from the window. And outside, lights from the shoreline hotels and houses shimmered in the chop.

We studied the menu, trying to synchronize a dish to fit our mood. My wife chose a sampler plate called "The Treasure Chest" while my son Bear, the gourmet, ordered a corn dog and fries. I settled on charbroiled oysters in the half-shell topped with marinara sauce.

While we waited, a waitress brought me an Anchor Steam beer, my wife an iced tea, and my son an orange juice.

Linda Rondstadt's torchy version of "What's New" drifted in from upstairs, serving as background for dinner forks knocking against plates, ice cubes tinkling in glasses and people chatting idly between mouthfuls.

Then the waitress brought us small bowls of New England clam chowder. I've had chowder in New England, and for my money, this is better. Almost velvety in texture, chunks of clams and potatoes swim in spicy stock.

First a spoonful of soup, then a bite of San Francisco-baked French bread spread thick with real creamery butter. When the bread's sourdough tang hits the tongue, angels sing hallelujah.

Then our dinners arrived. Steam rose from the oysters smothered in red sauce, and I squeezed lemon over the works. I slathered a baked potato with sour cream and chives, and buttered another hunk of bread.

The oysters, redolent with garlic and basil, melted on my palate, each bite as good as the last.

We ate and talked and drank in the view. A great meal.

Before leaving, we took a last stroll on the pier. Nadine and I walked hand in hand, with Bear clowning in front.

"I like it here, Dad," Bear said.

"Me too, son," I replied.

A Torrent Of Memories

Dressed in cutoff jeans and T-shirt, her long, brown hair knotted atop her head, my 19-year-old daughter, Tyra, went into her room, packed her things and left the nest Saturday morning.

"Don't worry, Dad, I'll be home a lot. I'm only going to Temecula," she said.

With her little blue hatchback, the one she calls "Bubba," groaning under the weight of her belongings, she drove off, heading out of my life and into her own.

Her moving out didn't come as a surprise, but that didn't make it any easier for me.

As I listened to her rummage through her closet, and heard the zip and unzip of baggage as she tossed clothes in, I couldn't help but reminisce about our lives together.

First, there were the months of hand-wringing as she gestated in her mother's womb. The tiresome nights when I tossed and turned, my stomach knotted with fear, praying: "Please, God, let her be healthy. Please, God, make everything all right. Please, God, watch over her."

And I would roll over, to **press** against my wife's back, and with my arm draped over her abdomen, I could feel my baby kicking and stretching inside her.

How very strange and wondrous it all was.

Tyra, I had never known joy like the joy I experienced when Dr. Stehley held you up like the catch of the day, proclaiming in his wry, Irish brogue, "Yep, she's a keeper. A real beaut."

142

And indeed you were. I'll never forget when they wheeled you out with your mother. Tiny purple fingers balled up into dainty fists. Thick, black hair crowning your head. Lips curled into a hint of a smile.

From the fourth-floor hospital window, snow-capped Palomar Mountain loomed in the distance, and your grandmother named you "Yuyushea," Snow Flower.

We brought you home to a small, single-wide trailer on our land behind Uncle Peanut's place. It was in there that I changed my first diaper. Not my idea of a good time, mind you, but I had no choice.

If you would have asked me when I was 19 if I thought I would ever be changing diapers, my answer would have been an unequivocal, "NO WAY!" But you just never know where life's going to take you.

You were born poor. Our trailer had no water heater, so we bathed you in water warmed in soup pots on top of the stove. And powdered you down with corn starch and wrapped you in a blanket with silk edging. For years, the "blankie" went where you went.

It was a great time for me, Tyra. Growing up, we read books together and watched Disney films and played peekaboo.

It wasn't all fun, however. The teething nights, when the only way to get you to sleep was to take you for long drives. The hospital nights when you'd get sick and we'd rush you to emergency rooms with a 105-degree fever. The time you fell on the Pepsi can and sliced the heck out of your little nose.

Or the time when we left you with the baby sitter when you were 5 and came home to find you weren't there. The baby sitter had let you show two creeps where somebody's house was and, hours later, you hadn't returned.

Wild-eyed, we called the cops and, thinking the worst, I loaded up my gun, laid it on the back seat and went looking for you.

Luckily, your cousins found those guys and whipped them soundly before I got to them. Feeling the way I was feeling, I would have willingly spent a lifetime in prison to get them if they had hurt you. Such are a father's feelings.

Yes, rearing you has been Mr. Toad's Wild Ride, Tyra. And the images keep flashing across my mind: Strapping you in the car seat with the nursery-rhyme characters printed on vinyl; your first softball game, you running out onto the diamond, baseball cap pulled down over your ears, lugging a fielder's glove almost bigger than you were; the yellow chicken suit for the tap-dance recital; the white-lace First Holy Communion dress; the first time I saw you in high heels; the nights of parental worry when you didn't come home on time from dates.

Take care of yourself, Tyra. Remember, I love you.

And, I'll still be praying, "God, please watch over my little girl."

Puppy Love Knows No Bounds, Dear

Deaf to my wife's snarls, I presented myself with a pup this Christmas.

Both my wife and our dachshund, Brittany, hate him. My wife especially. Immune to his charms, she chooses to recognize only his faults.

"Your dumb dog just pulled the sheets off the line."

"Your stupid mutt chewed up the hose."

"Your dopey dog dumped all over the driveway."

I try to defend him. "He's only a pup. He'll come around," I say as I'm raking up the Styrofoam cup he's strewn about the back yard.

Brittany barely tolerates him. She's accustomed to being queen of the place, and he plain and simple bugs her. She turns her back on him when he tries to play. She barely lets him on the rug where they sleep. Most of all, she despises his eating habits.

Brittany likes to linger over her food, daintily chewing each mouthful. The pup attacks his chow, burying his muzzle in the bowl like a badger after a ground squirrel, scattering about kibble. He empties his bowl in nanoseconds, so naturally he tries to horn in on hers.

But she won't share. She growls, "Get away from me, you disgusting pig."

He yips, "Ah, come on, can't I have some, please, huh, huh, please?"

She barks back, "Not on your life, loser."

On and on it goes.

I call him Griz, short for Grizzly. If you saw him, you'd know why. He's half chocolate lab, half German Shepherd, the first-born of a litter from the Rincon Indian Reservation. When I brought him home, he was a cinnamon brown powder puff with a stubby tail and floppy years. He looked just like a bear cub. Now about 6 months old, he's losing his puppy fluff, and his adult teeth are growing in, but he's still all pup.

He's gangly, like a teen-ager who's sprouted too fast. All feet, knees and elbows. He can't run and chew gum at the same time. I watch him play with the neighborhood dogs, roughhousing the way dogs do. He's forever slipping and falling, rolling in the dirt, scrambling to get his legs under him.

He's such a poser, too. When dogs wander into the yard, he stands and barks, like he's guarding his turf. The other dogs just laugh at him, waltz right in, drink his water, pee on his bushes and dare him to do something about it. If I walk out there, the other dogs will take off, and Griz will give chase, like he's the one scaring them off. When he comes back, grinning, little stub wagging, chest swelling, he acts like a somebody.

I'm sure he's the butt of many dog jokes with the local toughs. Probably call him Cream Puff, Pee Wee Herman and stuff. But he's just a pup.

Yesterday morning we went jogging, Griz and I. Brittany, currently in heat, is sequestered at a friend's house. So Griz and I went out on our own.

We took the dirt road behind our house, which winds past the old ballfield and crosses a dry creek bottom.

At first light, gray fog hovered about the treetops. The mist dampened his coat, pasting his puppy fringe to his jowls. Nose to the trail, he zigged and zagged through the rabbit trails, sniffing for game amid sage and buckwheat.

Up ahead I spotted a brush rabbit squatting on haunches. I wondered if Griz would notice. It took a while, but he eventually figured out something was up. He kicked it into gear.

The rabbit let him get close, teasing him, then sprang off in a leap. The rabbit chose an escape route up a steep creek bank, scurrying up the rocky path without a look back. Griz, nose full of rabbit, followed.

For a moment he looked like a hunter. Stretching out in full gallop, gobbling up the landscape, he actually built up speed. Griz hit the bank at full steam, got about halfway up, then toppled unceremoniously onto his back.

Like a colt standing for the first time, he got up, shook off the dust and just stood there, looking sheepish.

He trotted back to me. I patted him on the head. "It's OK boy, you're just a pup."

Steinbeck, Seals And Sandwiches

Somewhere beyond Bakersfield, on the long, lonely straightaway of I-5, our headlights carved a yellow hole into the night, pointing out the white lines that would lead us to my parents' house in San Jose.

"Hand me a sandwich, Bear," I said. My 10-year-old son, Bear, and I were alone in the truck on this first night of vacation. The rest of the family couldn't break free from work and would follow in a few days.

I bit into a sourdough sandwich of hard salami, dill pickles, purple onion and Monterey Jackcheese. With the opening jitters of the trip past, and the roadside distractions few, the time had come.

"OK, Bear, I want you to listen to this. You may not like it at first, but give it a chance. Pay attention. This is some of the greatest writing ever," I told him.

I slipped John Steinbeck's "Cannery Row" into the cassette player.

As we munched sandwiches, ate oranges and drank cream soda, Mack and the boys collected frogs, Doc in his laboratory sipped beer to Gregorian chants and a curious Chinese man flip-flopped down the wet Monterey streets during dusk's pearl-time.

And it was great floating along the highway, just Bear and me, in the soft green of the dashboard lights, listening to Monterey's Cannery Row come alive.

Several days later, we tooled down Highway 1 where it skirts along the coast, weaving between sand dunes and farmlands.

Straw-hatted field workers pulled weeds from row after row of bristling gray-green artichokes. Sunflowers, yellow petals wilted from too much sun, lined tilled fields. Flatbed trucks stacked with produce crates unloaded at a vegetable stand called The Thistle Stop.

We rolled with the highway from the farm country into the city, turning with the signs to Cannery Row and the Monterey Bay Aquarium. The streets teemed with cars and tourists.

Before exploring Cannery Row we visited Monterey's famous aquarium. A 20-minute line formed outside. In front of us, a dowdy woman with two chins rambled ad nauseam about how disgusted she was by the way new dress styles hung like sacks.

Inside the aquarium, full-size replicas of killer and gray whales dangled from the ceiling. People milled about everywhere, pointing out interests to fidgety children.

Monterey Bay ocean life darted and circled in million-gallon tanks. Sharks, sea bass, albacore, mackerel and more swam in silvery formations. Jellyfish floated like ghostly parachutes, their long, spindly tendrils flowing like ribbons from a party dress.

Outside on the observation decks, Bear and I slathered mustard on soft pretzels and ate while leaning over the rail overlooking the bay. Kayakers, whole gaggles of them, paddled amid the kelp beds and past sea rocks white with guano, where fat seals lounged like the rich and famous.

After several hours in the aquarium, we headed for Cannery Row. We blinked against the hard sunlight, searching for signs of what used to be. Not much. Cannery Row is a tourist haven. The canneries, once bustling with the sardine harvest, now house souvenir shops, taverns and fancy seafood restaurants.

So Bear and I headed for the wharf and took a path to the beach to wander in the shadows of the pilings where the tide lapped against concrete stanchions. Maybe Doc searched these same pilings for starfish, I told him.

Later, we found the John Steinbeck Spirit of Monterey Wax Museum and took in the waxen vignettes that started with the Indian history of Monterey Bay and ended with scenes from Steinbeck's "Cannery Row."

Bear saw Doc in his laboratory, Mack and the boys playing cards and Flora Woods, kindly madam of the Lone Star Cafe, shepherding her girls. It was as close as we could get to the old Steinbeck days.

Afterward Bear said, "You know, Dad, that really helped me see what the book was about." Then, before he fell asleep in the car, he said, "Thanks, Pop."

And I hoped he'd remember this as a good day.

Different Time, Different Place

Danny cycled. Born to a family of Kansas wheat farmers, Danny couldn't wait to pedal out of that land of bib overalls, tractor exhaust and fried chicken on Sundays to chase Olympic gold in the Golden State.

Peggy danced. She was reared Berkeley hip, the daughter of academic parents who allowed Peggy her uniqueness. She felt most at home in tights, in front of dance-studio mirrors, legs astraddle the barre.

Peggy and Danny met at the University of California, Santa Cruz. She majored in math; he needed help with equations. Their numbers added up.

Danny moved into Peggy's small bungalow near the beach. Inexpensive Indian tapestries covered the cracks in the plaster walls. A curtain of colored beads separated the kitchen from the living room. A thrift-store bookcase held the usual college fare: Jungian psychologies, Herman Hesse novels, the Kama Sutra, Sylvia Plath's "The Bell Jar."

At the time, 1971, I was going with Dyanna, also from the Bay Area, who befriended Peggy in theater class. By extension, Danny and I became friends as well.

One night, they had us over to dinner. Peggy cooked curried chicken and saffron rice. Danny poured green tea into mugs. We sat in the living room around a low table on big pillows and talked. Candles burned. An Eric Satie record played on the stereo.

It was a pleasant evening, but we left early. Danny, in training, had to rise before daylight to pedal his racing bike. He'd be back around noon. Did we want to get together later?

"I know a place," Danny said.

The next afternoon we climbed into Mr. Green, Dyanna's Volvo station wagon. Danny directed us - left here, right there - along forested Santa Cruz back roads.

We parked in a dirt pull-out and hiked a trail that led through a grassy meadow into a stand of redwoods. Once beneath the canopy of trees, the trail sidled a silver creek. About a half-mile upstream Danny pronounced our arrival.

"What do you think?" he asked.

Water sluiced down smooth, refrigerator-sized boulders into a sandy-bottomed pool, about 5-feet deep and maybe 20 feet across. Sun rays filtered through the towering redwoods, tinting the water an emerald green. Ferns sprouted through the cracks between boulders. Fish darted out of sight.

Free-thinking, emancipated Peggy made the first move.

"I'm going in," Peggy said. She flung off her blouse, unbuttoned her jeans and dived in. Her lithe dancer's body shot through the depths. She bobbed up, laughing, her long, black hair pasted to her white shoulders.

Color me surprised.

Not to be outdone, Dyanna shrugged out of her clothes and dived in, too, leaving the farm boy and the product of Catholic schools on the bank.

"Come on you two," goaded the girls.

An Irish grin broke across Danny's face. He shed his clothes, revealing his farmer's tan, now a racing-shorts tan, and followed suit.

That left me. Now, I had been an athlete. A veteran of countless locker-room showers. That kind of nudity didn't bother me. And I had been around the block with girls, so I was OK with that part. But I had never just willy-nilly disrobed before a woman I wasn't involved with, out in the open, in front of God and everyone.

A lifetime of words from stern-faced, black-robed priests and nuns burned into my ears - "Chastity, my son."

A load of catechism guilt dropped on me. "Was this sin?"

I hesitated. Sunlight filtered through overhead branches, as if through stained-glass windows. A breeze rustling through ferns sounded like turning prayer-book pages. The creek murmured in Latin.

"Whatchya waiting for. You're not chicken, are you?" they teased.

That tore it. Nobody calls me chicken, I told myself. My clothes were off in a flash, and I was in the water. Cold, cold water.

And we gamboled in the water for a time, nothing sexual, just children of nature. It seemed innocent enough. Yet exciting nonetheless.

Did I do wrong? I guess God only knows.

Gordon Johnson

Finding Peace Amid Garden's Memories

The wooden slats sagged under my weight as I sat on the bench in the patio gardens at the Pala reservation's Mission San Antonio.

I wanted a few moments of solitude. As I sat, the January sun sifted through palm fronds and pepper tree branches. Light and shadow played peekaboo on the red-tiled paths. Wide swathes of sunlight bleached the mission's white-plastered adobe walls.

I watched a mission cat - a furry black cat with a white chest and yellow eyes - leap atop a wagon wheel propped against the thick trunk of a pepper tree. Franciscan friars, no doubt, planted the tree nearly two centuries ago to spice up mission meals. I imagined the cracked peppercorns sprinkled into beef stew bubbling in cast iron pots suspended over the cooking fires.

The cat sat near a fork in the tree, her white-tipped tail swinging like a pendulum, her feline eyes intent on several sparrows chirping in nearby branches. The birds, taking notice of the cat, never got close enough. But the cat didn't discourage easily. She waited.

I look at myself and wonder if that's what I've done too much of my life. Bide time. Content to wait for something that will never come.

I've had good times here, though. Years ago, when my children fussed during Sunday Mass, I quickly volunteered to escort them outside. We made a beeline for the gardens, passing through the gift shop, where Bea Ornelas (who is still there) worked behind the counter.

I much preferred the breezy gardens to the stuffy church. So did my kids. Once we tasted freedom, we were hard **pressed** to return until Mass was nearly over. My wife scowled at our dalliances. We, however, reveled in them.

Little hands in my hand, we walked along the tiled paths, encountering all sorts of things to point out and talk about - statues of fat friars, colorful mosaics, terra cotta bird houses.

Potted plants of all sorts swung from the long, low porch supported by hand-hewn beams, now gray and weathered, but once tall evergreens atop Palomar Mountain.

Nailed to the beams were horseshoes and hoe heads so encrusted with rust they looked salvaged from the sea.

My kids loved the adobe-and-brick fountain, built in the shape of a hexagon, atop some brick steps. They'd run to the fountain and stick their heads over the sides to watch the fish. Then we'd toss in coins and make wishes. I wished my kids would grow up to live happy, fulfilled lives.

On this day, a big orange koi swam with transparent fins in the depths. Smaller goldfish followed, stopping now and then to suck up a delicacy from the algae bottom.

I found a quarter in my pocket and flipped it in. As it sank, I closed my eyes and wished my same wish.

Next to the fountain grows the grandfather lemon tree, its fruit gnarly and wrinkled like an old man's face.

And across the path from the lemon tree, near the ancient orange tree, is the small aviary, also a hexagon. Doves - some white, others brown, one gray - roost on dowels stuck into the cage wire. Their melancholy calls blend with the calls of hundreds of other birds flitting among the greenery.

Every time I roam the gardens, I vow I'm going to educate myself about plants and grow a garden of my own. I find these gardens so tranquil, so spiritually refreshing, that I want one like it at home. I have yet to make good on that vow, however. I'm strapped by laziness.

When I think of all the labor that went into this mission, I have mixed feelings. I envision the Indians mixing the mud, hauling the beams, stacking the adobes, and I shake my head at their hardships. The missionaries coerced Indians to work, while robbing Indians of their culture and lands.

It's not a pleasant history. But I believe you have to make the best of the history dealt to you.

So I come to the gardens to appreciate what my ancestors worked for. I hope they look down from the celestial heights to see the joy they have brought.

I want them to know their work wasn't for nothing.

Dishing Out Advice A Hazard Of Getting Older

The older I get the more I seem compelled to dish out advice to the young, as if my supposed acquired wisdom is a confection, a lip-smacking treat they should be pleased to receive.

Usually my advice is couched in stories of my younger, hipper days. I'll be sitting around a table populated with twentysomethings, when some kind of irresistible force grabs hold and before I know it, I'm regaling them ad nauseam with tales from the '60s.

Usually my stories begin with: "When you get to be my age you'll find ..." or "Back when I was your age ..." or "You guys have it easy compared to what we had back in my days. Why ..."

I mean, I know better. I should keep my trap shut. When I was 20 I didn't want some 46-year-old blowhard telling me about the wild times he had swing dancing to the Glenn Miller Band.

I can remember rolling my eyes and stifling yawns while a potbellied fogy reminisced in full flush about the fuzzy pink sweater Molly Sue wore the night of their prom.

Now I have the potbelly and I'm telling the stories. But living in the past seems to be the curse of old age. And it doesn't look like I'm going to escape its spell.

Most of us won't. I gotta believe Baby Boomers will be horrible bores, even worse than the World War II generation.

You see, deep down in the heart of the Baby Boomer there is the solemn, unshakable belief that we are the most enlightened generation ever to walk this planet.

We grew up in the '60s, when idealism reigned. Ours was a generation of thinkers. We embraced radical ideas. We hallucinated into unexplored worlds. We believed in nature. We rebelled against power brokers. We tasted freedom. Our women burned their bras, for crimney sakes. How much freer could you get?

I can actually remember sitting in a coffeehouse with friends, drinking French roast, smoking Gitane cigarettes and deriding the use of underarm deodorant as a crime against nature.

We'd say it was just another gray-flannel scheme to bilk the public. Corporate pigs conning us into believing we needed this roll-on or that spray deodorant so our body odors won't offend. Then we'd say that as humans, it is our nature to emit smells. It's natural. The odor is part of the way we fit into the order of the universe. Anyone who uses deodorant is a corporate dupe. Yes, really very plastic.

Similar conversations spewed forth on every college campus in America.

Weird. Yes. But we thought we knew what were talking about. You see, we read back then. Late into the night, with jasmine incense burning, we sipped green tea and read Alan Watts, Hermann Hesse, John Fowles, J.R.R. Tolkien and Carl Jung, with the Rolling Stones playing on reel-to-reel tape in the background.

And their ideas made us feel above it all. Better than the rest. Turned us into sprout-eating, earth-shoe-wearing, wheat-bread-baking, astral-projecting space cowboys. But what did it get us? What did we do with all this information? Where are we now?

You'll find most of us nestled deep into our Barcaloungers, remote control in hand, watching our wide-screen TVs, making snide remarks to our kids about what simpering idiots the Gen-Xers on "Friends" are, and how much cooler we were at that age.

It galls me, sometimes, to see what we've become - crass consumers.

What happened to our ideals? What happened to the anti-materialism we preached?

I'm no better. I spend way too much time daydreaming about driving a showroom-new, four-wheel drive, king-cab pickup with a bruiser engine, brushed aluminum rims and a matching camper shell.

There was a time when I would have thought such a pickup a gas-guzzling, environmental nightmare. Now I'm wondering how many speakers for the CD player I can cram into the cab.

Somehow I feel I've let myself down. I feel self-deflated. And I get a queasy feeling of guilt when I start drumming my chest to the kids about how great things were in the '60s.

I'm better off just keeping the old trap shut.

Desert Sands Are Blanket Of Solitude

The Anza-Borrego Desert in winter is like a quiet house. No motorized sounds, no voices, no click of heels on the kitchen floor. Only a smattering of birds gossiping from branches, and the wind's low moan careening through passes, interrupt the silence.

I'm alone, with no sense of loneliness. The landscape feels populated by spirits of the past - Indians, lost prospectors, hopeful immigrants, bearded desert rats who just preferred solitude.

From the elevations of Culp Valley along Highway S-22 in San Diego County, I navigate down a dry wash carved by rivulets from a recent rain, heading for Pena Springs. I see no footprints in the damp sand. No sign of anyone else, except for a discarded sock with the initials A.D.B. printed in permanent ink on the sole.

Did it fall out of his pack? Did he change clothes here and overlook it? Did foot-odor stink it up so bad he decided not to foul his other clothes with the smell? The desert gets you wondering about inconsequential things like that.

I button my denim jacket up to my neck against the chill. Black storm clouds roil over the jagged-toothed San Ysidro Mountains. But the western slopes often wring out the rain before reaching here, so it's not raining. It smells like rain though.

In places where I must cut through the brush, thorny plants called cat's claw scratch against me. Another mean-looking, spiny bush, like the kind you see in documentaries of the African plains, pokes through my jacket when I try to sneak past it. Lower to the ground, silver needles bristle from buckhorn cholla, a tubular cactus that sprouts everywhere.

The wildflowers haven't blossomed yet, leaving the terrain a muted gray. Gray sand, gray granite boulders, gray-green plants that hug the shade of taller sugar bush and smoke trees.

I arrive at the spring, a clear trickle of water that wriggles through a tangle of grasses and reeds.

I cross it and climb to an outcropping of boulders with a good view and sit for awhile. Rain water has collected in two grinding depressions atop a flat boulder. I reach in and touch the algae that flourishes at the bottom. It slips through my fingers like the cold spinach I left on my plate as a kid.

Indians usually mashed acorns in such depressions, but I'm willing to bet there's not an oak tree within 10 miles of Pena Springs. Instead, I figure chia seeds and mesquite beans were pulverized into flour here. I hear the women and girls singing as they work; their manos, their grinding stones, marking rhythm.

The desert in winter is time stilled. Peninsula Bighorn sheep, as they have for untold years, wander the great rocky crags that enclose this swale. I don't see them, but I suspect they see me. My grandfather told me stories of rams, 225-pounders with massive, curling horns, that he saw when he was a kid prospecting with his father in this land. I would like to see one, too, just so I would know how he felt.

Through a gap in the mountains, the desert floor spreads out into emptiness. A road here, a clump of buildings there, then miles of unending sand.

More mountains ascend on the other side of the desert, but I don't care to imagine what's beyond them.

I just want to sit here for awhile, breathe in and out, and listen to my heartbeat. I close my eyes to drink it all in.

It's nearly dusk as I get up to leave. Darkness envelopes the land by degrees. The round moon, white as sun-bleached cattle bones, plays amid drifting clouds. And as I make my way back to my truck, darkness begins to transform chaparral and boulders to silhouettes.

For a moment, I worry that I might not find the main trail again, but after 100 yards of working through criss-crossing paths I spot the waffle-print of my hiking boots in the sand. My truck isn't far now.

The turnaround where my truck is parked is bordered by buried telephone poles cut waist high. As I walk by one of the poles, I notice someone has taken the time to arrange pebbles into some kind of design. I look closer and see it's a peace sign.

The desert in winter is a peaceful house.

Finding Your Ancestral Self

Dear Brandon,

Well, son, you're 16 now. I can't believe 16 years have disappeared since the delivery-room nurse handed you to me and said, "Well, you've got your fullback!"

I cradled you in my arms, all 10 pounds of you, your face scrunched up, your unsure fingers grasping for mine, and I felt the immediate bond a father has for his son. Blood of my blood. Flesh of my flesh. Life of my life. My heart swelled with love for you.

I raced home and asked Grandpa Hepa, as you later called him, what to name you. He looked inward for a moment and then said, "Kahel. Name him Kahel. It means scout quail. That way he can grow to be a leader for the people."

And grow you did. Now, you're taller than I am. And, in many ways, better.

I haven't told you often enough, but you've made me proud, son. You've become a fine peon player. I fill with pride to see you kneel down with your team and play the game the way it should be played - with honor and respect.

You've become a fine bird-singer. Your rattle sounds true. Your voice resonates with tradition. You've gotten so accomplished, our roles have reversed. Now, you are the teacher, and I'm the student.

But most of all, I'm proud see that your heart is good. You care. You don't always think of yourself first. To me, this is genuine strength. Of this, I am most proud.

Now that you are 16, and on your way to manhood, I want to say a few things before you reach the age when you'll discount everything I say.

It is natural for you to seek independence. The time has come for you to make your own life decisions. But as your father, a father who loves you, I want to share some words I believe to be true. These words, if you take them to heart, will help you to live in a good way.

You were born and reared on the Pala Indian Reservation. In your veins courses the blood of the ancestors. What you do with your life reflects on all, past and present, who have contributed to your existence. You have an obligation not to shame them.

In the sweat lodge we often talk about "walking the Red Road." What exactly is the Red Road? I believe the Red Road is the path toward balance in life, toward harmony with the universe, toward oneness with the Creator. I believe it is the path toward morality, integrity and good works. I believe it is the path toward self-fulfillment, self-actualization and happiness.

The first step on that path is self-discovery. You must look into yourself to fathom the mysteries of your soul. Listen to the beat of your heart. Feel it thump with your life. Listen to the winds. They speak the secrets of Mother Earth. Look to the stars to see your place in the natural order. Maybe this sounds like metaphysical mumbo jumbo, but I guarantee that if you pay heed, your life will be fuller for it.

And remember, this is not something you do for 15 minutes and call it done. Self-awareness is a lifelong thing.

The next step on the path is moderation. I believe life is to be celebrated with a throw-back-your-head-and-howl-at-the-moon kind of joy. The Creator has provided many things for our pleasure. But the trick is to enjoy without excess. Too much of anything will undo you. And one must earn pleasures. Work that contributes to the common good is the staple of moderation. Fun is the dessert. In your life, work and play should be done in equal measure.

The next step is actually three steps in one. I call them the three D's - desire, determination and discipline. Desire to achieve. Find what it is you love to do, then embrace it with your whole being. Be determined to achieve. Life can be harsh and unfair. You will be knocked down many times. But you must get up. Never, never, never quit. Discipline yourself to excel. The world is competitive. You must be at your best to do your best.

Lastly: Love God. Love yourself. Love people. Love life.

You may not understand all this. But if you stick to these words, you will have a shot at happiness. And, son, that is all I have ever wanted for you - true happiness.

Love, Dad.

Lover's Lane Leap of Faith

I stood, with my thumb out, at the on-ramp of Highway 1 in Santa Cruz. It was spring of 1970, and the perfume of lilac, wisteria and apple blossoms sweetened the air. Sunlight glinted off car windshields. Sea gulls winged toward the ocean. It was a swell morning, but not for me.

My mood was dark. Jealousy gripped me by the throat. I suspected my girlfriend had carried on with a UC Santa Barbara English professor the weekend before. I had never met him, but she had mentioned him in passing as a former lover. I pictured him bearded, with wire-rimmed glasses and a tweed jacket. He probably drove an English sports car. I bet he quoted William Blake in tender moments to my girl. My girl.

Green-eyed, full of bile, I just wanted to wander. Flee my pain. I pleaded with cars for a lift.

A maroon Peugeot pulled over. I piled into the back seat.

From behind the wheel, a bearded man asked: "Where ya headed?"

"It doesn't matter much," I said.

"We're going to Esalen," he said. He wore a black beret and smoked a pipe. A woman in a long denim skirt and a peasant blouse smiled next to him.

"Sounds good to me," I said.

We took off. He turned up the radio a bit. A string quartet played a sullen piece I didn't recognize. We drove south on what may be the world's most beautiful highway. Monterey pines loomed roadside. Fishing boats bobbed in the bay. Straw-hatted farm workers stooped in artichoke fields. I tried but failed to enjoy the scenery.

Up front, the couple talked, paying no attention to me. But that was OK. I had nothing to say anyway.

I gathered they were off to Esalen for some kind of couples therapy. I figured they would sit around naked in hot tubs, sip white wine and explore inner feelings. I hated that touchy-feely stuff.

I pulled my journal from my backpack and tried to write against the motion of the car. It was like that the whole ride. Them talking. Me writing.

They dropped me at the Esalen turn-off, leaving me alone on Highway 1.

My next ride came in a beat-up turquoise 1956 Chevy. A long-haired guy in leather pants and a thermal-underwear shirt waved me inside. Credence Clearwater sang from an eight-track tape.

"I'm going to Santa Barbara," he said. "But I have to stop at this dude's house for a while."

"Fine with me," I said. Santa Barbara. Scene of the crime.

This guy was a talker. He delivered a 100-mile monologue of inanities. As he prattled, I stared out the window, admiring the houses we passed. Wood-shingled, multi-decked, with stained-glass windows, they perched like poetry on the bluffs overlooking the Pacific. Would I ever have a house like that? Fat chance.

We stopped at a weathered farmhouse that resembled a Crosby, Stills and Nash album cover. The living room reeked of spilt wine and stale hashish. A guy in a T-shirt emerged from a bedroom. Money and a package changed hands. I should have known. A dope deal. I clenched my fist all the way to Santa Barbara, checking the mirrors for cops.

He left me off downtown and I roamed the Santa Barbara streets, oblivious to their charm. I checked into a wino hotel; $5 for a room with the bathroom down the hall. I slept in my clothes on stained bed sheets. An old-timer in the next room hacked like a lunger all night.

The next morning, I took a city bus to UC Santa Barbara. I walked amid the buildings of academia, all glass and angular concrete. I studied the faces of people carrying books, wondering if one of them was the joker who had been with my girl.

For lunch, I had a torpedo at a college hangout called the Yellow Submarine. The gutted Bank of America, firebombed by student protesters the year before, stood boarded up across the street.

That afternoon, I rode a Greyhound back to Santa Cruz. That night, I talked to my girlfriend. She swore nothing happened between her and the professor.

I decided to believe her. Life was too bleak otherwise.

Real Indian Movies Finally Being Made

With red licorice and caramels stuffed into back pockets, we padded across the theater carpet into the darkened stadium seating of Temecula's The Movie Experience.

My sons, Brandon and Bear, and I had come to see "Smoke Signals," a movie unlike any we had ever seen before. An Indian movie made by Indians.

The movie is based on an excerpt from Sherman Alexie's collection of short stories, "The Lone Ranger and Tonto Fistfight in Heaven." Alexie, 31, a Spokane-Coeur d'Alene Indian, wrote the screenplay and Chris Eyre, 28, a Cheyenne-Arapaho, directed it.

For those of you unaware of Alexie, I recommend him. His writing is hard-edged realism softened by poetry-induced illusion. At times he's a fist slammed into a windshield, a beer bottle shattered against a street sign, a T-shirt stained with wine.. Other times, he's the face of an elder in lake mists, the mysterious voice in wind-swept evergreens, the ascension of hope in a graceful two-handed dunk in the hoop.

He transforms words into music. Born hydrocephalic, Alexie had brain surgery as an infant and wasn't expected to live. He survived, but was a sickly youth who read voraciously to escape his infirmities. He read Steinbeck at age 5.

Later he channeled his lifelong reading into writing poetry and literature. And now movie-making.

169

I loved "Smoke Signals." Not one car chase. No shootouts with drug dealers. No gratuitous sex. Instead, the film relies on character development, witty dialogue and poignant storytelling to carry it.

While the film is rife with inside jokes, the predominately non-Indian audience I sat with laughed in the right places, so I think the message got across.

And what is the message? It's simple - Indians are people, too. Not every Indian is a shaman. Not every Indian is a vision seeker. And on the spectrum's other end, not every Indian drinks to imbecility. Alexie describes the middle ground between noble and ignoble savage where most Indians can be found.

And too, the movie shows how far things have come from the days Jay Silverheels, a Shakespearian-trained actor, "ughed" his way through dialogue as Tonto.

Just having "Smoke Signals" play at a Temecula theater marks something of a milestone for Indian people. It's great for local Indians to be able to walk into a neighborhood theater and see other Indians on the big screen, acting as genuine Indians, not as Hollywood stereotypes.

More and more Indians are making their mark in the film industry.

Pechanga is also bringing in another film written, produced and directed by Indians. It's also the first film ever financed in its entirety by an Indian tribe.

Friday at 7 p.m., "Naturally Native" will play in the Pechanga Bingo Pavilion. Admission is free but donations are requested.

I haven't seen "Naturally Native," but I have read several reviews that say it's outstanding.

Valerie Red-Horse, a former UCLA film student who went on to act in many TV series, including "Murder, She Wrote," "Perry Mason" and "Anything But Love," grew frustrated with stereotypical Indian roles offered by studios.

Red-Horse decided to write her own movie. Too busy to carve out major blocks of time, she wrote in snatches, typing out scenes on her laptop between meetings and while waiting in airports.

She wrote a funny, yet realistic, story about three sisters trying to start a business selling Native American cosmetics. It's a mildly political film depicting the cultural challenges the sisters faced in the non-Indian business world.

Red-Horse knew no mainstream studio would finance this departure from the sex and violence of formula pictures. So with script in hand, Red-Horse pitched her vision to the Mashantucket Pequot tribe, a successful gaming tribe in Connecticut.

They gave her $800,000. She made a movie.

Thank you, Alexie and Red-Horse, for helping to break the chain of low Indian expectations. Now my kids, and all Indian kids, can see that if they believe, they can achieve.

Spooky Legends To Live By

In daylight, Deadman's Hole seems safe enough. Songbirds jump from cattail to cattail like gymnasts working the uneven bars. Spring water seeps from underground aquifers to nourish the swamp root and tules. Willow and oak branches shake hands in the midday breeze.

But at night, Deadman's Hole is no place to play. Just off Highway 79 about 7 miles northwest of San Diego County's Warner Springs, bad things may have happened in this remote, mountain area.

According to "Haunted Places: The National Directory," by Dennis William Hauck, in 1858 a man was found beaten to death here. In 1870, a Frenchman was attacked in his nearby cabin. In 1888, the mutilated bodies of a prospector and a young woman were found. That same year a pair of hunters discovered a cave littered with human bones. In 1922, a man was found with his neck broken. Not long afterward, an Indian girl was found similarly brutalized.

Hauck wrote the primary suspect in these killings was a family of Sasquatch-like creatures - big, hairy, bloodthirsty beings - that roamed the countryside in search of fresh kill.

The hunters who found the bone-littered cave claimed a ferocious, apelike monster attacked them. They escaped only after firing shots at it.

To me, it sounded like maybe these mountainfolk nipped a little too often at the hard cider. But, curious, I called Tony Tobin, a Temecula historian, who grew up in Chihuahua Valley not far from Deadman's Hole.

Tobin, 84, said he couldn't recall ever hearing about the Sasquatches in that territory. Tony's older brother, Art, said he remembered something about a man being found dead there. That's how the place got its name. And he vaguely recalled a woman being killed there as well.

Sasquatch? Naw.

But many Indians believe.

A buddy of mine, Leroy Miranda, curator of the Cupa Cultural Center in Pala, and I drove up to Deadman's Hole the other day (and I underline day) to scope it out.

On the way up, we talked about how Indian people feel about things that go bump in the night.

Leroy believes the local Sasquatches may be Taqwish in disguise. Taqwish has long been a malevolent force in Indian Country. All sorts of stories and legends about him abound. In all of them, Taqwish is not to be meddled with.

"Taqwish is a shape-shifter, like a Skinwalker," Leroy says. Some say he once was a human being, who stole children and ate them, leaving only gnawed-on bones behind. So the people banished him. Now he is a spirit being, often taking the shape of ball lightning, whirlwinds and mothers-in-law (just kidding).

"But he can also be a Sasquatch," Leroy says. Leroy's mother, Donna, says she saw one peeking through creek willows on the Pala Indian Reservation in north San Diego County. Tall, hairy, red-eyed and foul-smelling, the beast scared the bejesus out of her.

Leroy believes they use riverbeds and creek beds to travel through Indian Country.

You can't spend much time in Indian Country, before the spooky stories spill forth. Indians around here often speak of the Little People, the leprechaun-like trolls that like to torment people. No, I shouldn't say that. Not all are bad. Leroy tells of an old woman who lived alone in the back country of the Santa Ysabel Indian Reservation near Lake Henshaw in San Diego County, who got too sick to leave her bed. Near death with weakness, she said, the Little People came to her aid, cooking her broth, giving her cool water to drink and sponging her forehead. They were good.

Most Little People aren't so nice, however. Most have wide, snaggly-toothed grins and laugh wildly at humans after bedeviling them.

Indian people know many such creatures of the night. They talk of the Sandman, a tall man all in black who peeks through windows. They talk of hoof-footed men, the men bred of evil, that hitchhike on lonely roads. And they talk of Taqwish, and who knows what shape he might take?

My advice. Tread lightly this Halloween night. And stay out of Deadman's Hole.

Corrals Empty, Cowboy Still Full Of Stories

He stood, a bit bent, waiting at his front gate, while his wife, Tina, undid the padlock.

He wore a faded Levis jacket, 501s and a white Stetson, and when he smiled, his blind left eye stared right past me.

Eighty-nine-year-old Danny Gallegos stuck out a hand, "You the newspaper man?"

"Yep," I said.

"So, you're that nosy guy," he said, with a laugh.

"Yep," I said.

"Come on in," he said to me and Forrest Green, the retired private investigator from Perris who introduced me to Danny.

We followed Danny into his old ranch house while a mean-eyed chow sniffed my pant leg.

Danny bought this 5-acre place in Nuevo for $37,000 back in 1947. Most years, the corrals out back held horses. Before that, he cowboyed in New Mexico. Danny is a throwback to a different time and place, where a man never walked if he had a horse; where fists, not lawsuits, settled disputes; where nothing was quite so sweet as a smooth-gaited horse.

With a groan, he lowered himself into a straight-backed chair at his dining room table, where a half-eaten pumpkin pie sat next to a Lazy Susan crowded with prescription medicine.

Tina, his Guatemalan wife who speaks little English, boiled water for coffee and turned to a Spanish-language TV station in the next room.

Danny speaks English with the lilt of a man whose first language is Spanish. He can't hear well, and he's had two strokes, so his memory wanders at times. But he tells stories with true relish, the mark of a born storyteller. With coffee poured, the stories commenced.

"I had a funny kind of a life when I was young. I was a cowboy from as far back as I can remember. When I was too young to ride alone, I used to fall asleep in my father's arms while he sat in the saddle," Danny said.

Danny grew up in the small New Mexico town of Bluewater, near the foothills of the Zuni Mountains.

"We lived two or three miles from town, which was just one store and a saloon," he said. "You could buy a little food there, not much, and shoes for horses and such. In the evenings the men gathered at the saloon to drink beer and play horseshoes."

By age 5, he worked cattle with his father from atop a horse. The horse was so tall that, to climb off, he looped his quirt around the saddle horn, then slid down it.

Schooling in the back country was a sometime thing, with a teacher who came now and again. "Other kids used to go to school. I was too busy with the cattle," he says. Danny never learned to read or write, and he kicks himself for it today.

But he preferred working with his father to school books.

"He was a tough man, but a good man," Gallegos said, pointing to the yellowed photograph of Severo Gallegos on the living-room wall. In the portrait, his father peered out with fiery eyes from beneath a wide-brimmed cowboy hat. Two pistols and a cartridge belt were at his waist.

Even as a kid, Danny could cut and earmark cattle as good as any man. He could stick on just about any horse. He could reach in and take a stillborn calf from its mother. By 14, he earned a man's wages.

As a teen-ager, Danny, who thought himself pretty quick with his dukes, stepped into the boxing ring for a bout with a traveling boxer.

The boxer worked Danny's face to a pulp. The fight left Danny blind in his left eye and kept him out of World War II.

In 1943, in search of more pay, Danny left New Mexico to work as a longshoreman in San Pedro. In 1947, he moved to Nuevo. He eventually retired as a union man, but all the while he kept up his cowboy ways: working local cattle, roping in rodeos, caring for his own stock.

On this day, he stands in his yard, where pigeons flutter in a nearby coop, but where the corrals are silent. "In all of life I loved horses the most. I loved everything about them," he said. "On a Saturday evening, this yard would be filled with men on horseback. Now, no one comes to see an old man. You come back any time."

I told him I would.

Gordon Johnson

Mirror Image: Like Mother, Like Daughter

My granddaughter, Sukmal Turner, turns 2 today.

It's been fascinating to watch Suki emerge as a person. In just two years, she's gone from a scrunched-up organism who spent most of her day sleeping, sucking and soiling diapers to a fun-loving, energy-packed, little human being.

What strikes me most is how much of my daughter, Tyra, I see in her. The way Suki runs up to me and purses her lips to give me a hello kiss sends me reeling back to when my daughter did the same.

The way her fingers wrap around her small spoon as she digs into a container of yogurt. The way her fine, straight hair flounces about her shoulders when she runs. The way her laughter fills the room. These all remind me of my daughter.

When Tyra was about Suki's age, we spent $200, a princely sum then, on our first good camera. A wannabe photographer, I practiced on Tyra, focusing the lens, measuring the light, looking for the perfect shot. I got to know my daughter's face through the viewfinder. The curl of her lips, the squint of her eyes, the flare of her nose when she smiled.

Back then, I belonged to a darkroom club. I developed my own film and printed from the negatives. I spent untold hours watching my daughter's face come to life in the printing paper as I agitated the chemical baths. I found great joy in those hours.

We still have those pictures, 8-by-10s of Tyra making a mess with dinner, Tyra taking a bath, Tyra asleep.

I miss those days with my kids, back when they thought I was all that. I loved sitting with them and reading from the Disney books we bought from a book-of-the-month club. For me, reading time was show time. I modulated my voice to sound like Mickey, Goofy, Donald Duck, even Minnie. Maybe I wasn't the best, but my kids still laughed.

When Tyra was Suki's age we often showered together. I taught my daughter her first peon songs in the shower. And we sang duets of "Bobby McGee" and "Old Paint" and "Help Me Make It Through the Night" to the rhythm of the shower spray drumming against the stall. I bet Tyra still remembers the lyrics to some of those songs.

I loved our long walks along the back roads of Pala. She drank in the landscape with unbounded curiosity, and I tried my best to explain how sun and rain nourished the sage plants we burned to purify ourselves. I pointed out the lizard tracks in the sandy washes and showed her how different the snake tracks looked. I showed her the veins in the sycamore leaves, the glitter of quartz in the river rocks, the tangle of orange widow's hair in the laurel sumac branches.

And the afternoon breezes lifted our laughter and gentle talk skyward. I believe it's still on its way to some distant star.

I liked the quiet Sunday mornings when I mixed pancake batter from scratch for Tyra and we ate while the rest of the house slept.

I liked when she fell asleep in the bed next to me while we watched TV in the small trailer where we lived back then.

I liked taking Tyra to the beach, and watching her run screeching when the icy water foamed around her toes. And then we walked the shoreline, her taking three or four steps to my one, hunting for sea shells.

"Look, Tyra, a sand dollar," I said.

And she'd scamper to wrest it from the wet sand. Her eyes would light up as she studied the shell's design.

"That's God's money," I told her.

Now, I rarely see my daughter. Although she lives in Rincon and works in Pechanga, both not far from Pala where I live, our schedules don't match. Our lives just don't intersect much.

And that's sad. It's sad how in our pursuit of large-screen TVs, digital stereos, sleeker cars and deeper carpeting we lose touch with loved ones. I'm just as much to blame. Plain fact is I'm **busy** . She's **busy** . And time is scarce.

But as Suki gets older, I hope Suki and I will do things together so I can relive some of those times I had with Tyra.

I want to see Suki's face when she catches a fish, when she blows on a dandelion and the white down parachutes into the wind, when she blows out the two birthday candles on her cake.

Happy birthday, Suki!

Digging Yourself Out Of Blackness On A Spring Day

I've returned from my walk and kicked off my boots to wriggle my toes in freedom. I've filled my cup with ice water and swallowed deeply. I've loaded a Michael Bloomfield CD and I'm listening to slick blues riffs. I'm seated at my desk writing this.

On my walk, I followed the barbed-wire fence to the creek bed that snakes along the bottom land behind my trailer on the Pala Indian Reservation.

On the way, I trampled through wild oats still green from recent showers. I passed thick colonies of prickly pear cactus growing beneath chinaberry trees. I sunk my heels into the soft dirt mounded by burrowing animals.

Pacific breezes airlifted the perfume of purple lilac blossoms. Songbirds fluttered amid budding trees. In the distance, horseshoes clanged against pegs. A wave of self-pity swept through me.

Spring. It's spring dang it. In the village, menfolk, no doubt with beers in hand, threw horseshoes and joked with each other. They were having fun.

What was I doing? Wandering alone, trying to dispel the blackness that pressed against my heart.

I stopped to study light and shadow angle across racquet-sized cactus pads. Small, rosy blooms bristled with promises of future cactus apples. New pads, tender with a wet-green skin, sprouted too. Here and there, last season's cactus apples - dusty and desiccated - clung tenuously to life. But soon, they too would fall.

181

I am felled by the pain of parenthood. What to do? I didn't expect my brood to be from The Donna Reed Show. But I didn't expect my teenagers to push me to the brink, either. Out all night, partying. No phone call. No: "Don't worry, Dad, I'm OK."

I am hurt. I am angry. I am frightened. I am a teardrop. I am a clenched fist. I am dark anxiety in broad daylight. I don't deserve this.

I slow myself down against downhill momentum as the path descends to the creek bed.

I have seen this creek rage in winter. Once it picked up a fire truck and upended it. Men almost drowned trying to rescue other men stranded on the truck. But this year, the creek is waterless. Last year's algae has dried into leathery patches that look like cow pies in the brown sand.

"My love for my children will never dry up like this creek," I tell myself. I love my children unconditionally. Nothing they do could make me stop loving them. That is a forever truth. But it doesn't mean I always approve.

I'm the father hawk watching his fledglings flap their wings for first flight. Will they fly or thud to the ground? I don't know. I can encourage, I can warn, I can talk till I'm parched. But I can't fly for them. I can't live their lives for them. Must let go. Let go. Let go.

A green-tinted lizard does push-ups on a gray log. His prehistoric snout points skyward, his reptilian eyes rove in their sockets. Other lizards, their backs a patchwork of geometric designs, scramble over deadwood. Their tiny claws scrape over the weathered grain.

All I ever wanted was for us all to be happy. This planet is not our home. We are but wayfarers here. Short-timers on the road to God knows where. So let's make the best of it while we're here. Life is too short for melodramatics.

A blue ribbon stretches across the creek bed. Attached to the ribbon is what's left of a blue party balloon. Some kid's party balloon, deflated and brittle like an old man's skin, rotting away in the creek bed.

Sure kids, party down. Nothing wrong with good times. Nothing amiss in shared laughter. But life isn't a continuous party. Can't be. If it is, it pops like that party balloon.

The value of life is measured by our contributions to the common good. That doesn't mean picking up the tab for a kegger. It means living up to our potential so we can help others live up to theirs.

A green-breasted hummingbird stops its wings for a moment to land on a scrub-oak twig. It rests for the briefest second, then launches itself again.

Our lives when clocked by geological time are less than a hummingbird's rest. It's all up to us.

Back in the trailer, I write these thoughts down to feel better. It works.

Long Trip Gives A Glimpse Intoa Father's Eyes

In the spring of 1960, we ordered summer clothes from the Sears catalog.

Traveling clothes. Lord have mercy, the Johnsons were going on vacation.

Before that, I'd never been on vacation. You see, for about two years, from when I was about 2 until I was 4, I never saw my father while he battled tuberculosis in a military hospital.

To a young boy, the red scar that slashed down my father's back was about the most exciting thing about him.

After doctors declared him fit, he emerged from the hospital and re-entered my life.

I had been living at my grandparents house on the Pala Indian Reservation with my mother and sister.

I slept in my Uncle Copy's bedroom, where pictures of boxers and ballplayers covered the walls. I ate when hungry, played when the mood struck, combed my hair if I felt like it and pestered my grandfather around the yard with never a rebuke.

I lived in freedom. That is, until my father arrived. In short order, he packed us up and moved us to Santa Clara where he attended college, and I learned to be civilized.

My father drilled us in table manners. It mattered to him which way the sheets unrolled from the toilet paper. He expected teeth to be brushed, hair to be combed and faces to be scrubbed. I even ate dreaded creamed cod on toast. "People who don't eat are sick, and sick people go to bed," he said. It was creamed cod or the pillow.

To enforce his will, he carved a paddle from an oak plank and kept it handy above the refrigerator. With one move toward the paddle, he could reduce us kids to stuttering idiots.

Frankly, I resented my dad for stealing me from my easy reservation life. I loathed his rules and manners and morality. His starched, button-down world reeked of structure and discipline. I much preferred the sweet scent of fresh tortillas and lazy reservation days.

Though I made frequent returns to the reservation, they only made my Santa Clara life seem more dismal.

During his college years, my dad spent most of his time hitting the books. Oh, he popped in to make sure I downed my greens and chewed with my mouth closed, but I didn't see much of him.

Then he graduated and wanted to take us on vacation, a road trip through the western states.

Enclosed in a car with mom, dad, and my three siblings - especially since my brother Paul was famous for getting car sick - wasn't my idea of a good time. But I had no choice.

My dad loaded up a yellow 1954 Plymouth station wagon powered by a flathead, six-cylinder engine. He hitched up a small teardrop trailer, the kind where the back end lifts up to reveal a kitchen. He lashed some trunks onto the roof-rack and we hit the blue highways to see America.

For about a month and half, we drove up California to the Pacific Northwest, up into British Columbia, down through Montana and states south.

We stopped in campgrounds for the night and ate lots of hard-boiled eggs on the road. The smell of eggs on vinyl upholstery still unsettles me.

But the main thing was, I got to know my dad on that trip. I watched him. I saw his pale eyes reflected in the rearview mirror. I noted his smiles, his conversational tone, his interest in showing us the countryside.

In Nevada, we stayed for a couple of days in a campground near some mountains. The kids played while my dad fixed the trailer tire.

In Oregon and Washington, we visited his relatives and saw the house where he was born. It made him more human somehow.

In New Mexico, we camped by a river and my dad scrambled us eggs and kippered snacks.

When traveling through the desert, with the sun parching our throats, we stopped at a gas station. My dad made sure all of us had cold pop before he bought himself a drink. When it came to him, only a warm chocolate drink was left. Yet he didn't complain.

Before the trip, I had my doubts. But afterward, I knew my dad loved us.

Moseying Through The Summer

I was a kid just looking for stuff to do.

To escape summer's fierceness, when the heat waves undulated like belly dancers above Pala Mission Road, I often headed for the shade of the corral.

Along Highway 76 where the Pala Indian Reservation houses stopped and eucalyptus and oak trees ascended with tangles of wild grapes clinging to lower branches, it was cool.

Back there, a couple of hogs wallowed in the mud in a makeshift pen. Mud caked to their black and white undersides as they grunted and squirmed to get deeper in the muck, and yellow jackets hovered and then gentled down for a landing in the slime.

"Stay away from the hogs," I had heard my grandfather say. So I minded not to get too close. But from the fat, lazy looks of the pigs I doubted they could even get up to attack. But I kept my distance all the same.

Some turkeys roamed the outgrowth back there. You could all the time find feathers on the ground. I made darts by sticking the feathers into the soft core of dried corncobs and threw them into the sky. I liked the way the cob darts rotated and wobbled on the descent.

Sometimes on hot days, I'd make a fan of the feathers. I liked the way the wind cooled the beads of sweat collected across my nose.

Past the tin barn, standing in a canopy of shade in his corral, stood Doughboy, my Uncle Jimmy Bank's white horse.

I was a young boy, and he was the horse of my daydreams. I saw myself atop him galloping along desert roads chasing after bad guys. I was on his back, with a Winchester rifle in the scabbard alert for an elk or a deer. I ran him to first place in important races. I didn't need to tie him at nights when we camped out on the trail.

He stood there magnificent, white and regal in a young boy's eye. His ears shifted to acknowledge my arrival. He shook off flies with a twitch of his withers then shuffled toward me.

I picked fresh grass and held it out for him to nibble. I knew enough to hold the grass in the palm of my hand so Doughboy wouldn't bite my fingers by mistake. He took the grass with a nod and munched. I petted his neck.

Doughboy was my Uncle Jimmy's parade horse. Every Corpus Christi, the mission festival commemorating the body of Christ, my Uncle Jimmy saddled Doughboy to lead the procession.

On those Sunday mornings, I would fall in behind the crowd that followed the priest and Uncle Jimmy as they wound through the reservation. The priest carried holy water in a bucket to sprinkle on front-yard altars laden with statues of saints.

As the priest blessed the saints, Doughboy would stand at attention as if sanctifying the proceedings. My Uncle Jimmy wore an eagle-feather headdress and carried the American flag, and I was proud of them both.

One day, my uncle spotted me hanging around the corral and asked, "Hey, Boy, you wanna ride Doughboy?"

Did I ever. My uncle didn't have a saddle small enough for me, so he just put me on bare back.

I can still smell my uncle's aftershave as he lifted me. I shifted around Doughboy's wide back to get comfortable. And then my uncle handed me the reins.

My first time on a horse. My uncle held onto Doughboy and led me around the corral. I felt the motion and the muscle in Doughboy's walk. Well, it wasn't a gallop across the desert, but it was something nonetheless.

From that point on, I could tell people, even brag, that I had ridden a horse. I never rode him again. He was my uncle's horse, and my uncle didn't cotton much to others riding him.

I understood, even back then, that getting to ride him was a rare thing.

Both Doughboy and my Uncle Jimmy lived to be old. They are both long dead. And I believe, that somewhere, they're still on parade.

On Birthdays, There's Often A Surprise

Sunday afternoon, I sit in the September heat in a hard-backed chair in front of my trailer.

A breeze teases the leaves of my Uncle Peanut's fruit and chinaberry trees next door. Across the way, I look out onto the field where my Aunt Inez's husband, Clifford Moss, once farmed watermelons. Although, probably in his 80s now, I still see him out there on occasion, disking the soil with his tractor to keep the weeds at bay.

Nothing stirs at the Nelson household, my other neighbors. Young Wayne Nelson played peon all night at the Morongo powwow, so I expect he's trying to sleep.

The Nelsons' little brown dog picks his way through my field, head low, tail wagging. He's come over to say hello. He rests his muzzle on my knee. I give his head a pat and his tail thumps involuntarily.

I pop the tab on a tall-boy of Miller Lite, take a drink to wish myself "Happy Birthday."

While I wasn't looking, 48 snuck up behind and grabbed hold. Nevertheless, I celebrate. I've gotten to the age, when birthdays are celebrated with a wistful smile instead of a raucous night.

"Ouch!!! Son of gun," I scream out. A red ant has sunk his fiery jibs into my ankle and it stings like a hot match head.

I brush him off and pour a little beer onto the bite. Not much alcohol in beer, but I figure it beats nothing. At least it's cool.

Kind of how the beer soothes the sting of another birthday.

Birthdays always give me the heebie-jeebies. Regrets flood in — another year without writing a book, another year without sailing to Tahiti, another year closer to the grave.

I take another swallow.

The cloudless sky is the blue of a faded work shirt. The little brown dog crawls under my trailer for shade. A yellow jacket buzzes toward his nest of honeycombed mud hanging beneath the trailer's awning.

Griz's water bowl is empty. Green algae in the bowl has caked dry. Most of the water has evaporated from the plastic tub where I bathed him. I haven't bothered to unlock the front door.

I could be watching softball games at the Pechanga Indian Reservation. Or I could be sitting on a hay bale in Morongo where feathered Indian dancers move moccasined feet in time to the drums. Or I could be walking on the Oceanside pier with my son, Bear, watching surfers ride the sea-green swell.

I could be anywhere but here. Yet here I am, sitting on a chair, by myself.

I take a few more gulps.

I savor each sip like it will be my last. Because it will be. Birthdays have traditionally been my time to jump on the wagon, and this year will be no different. Birthday beer, followed by a long abstinence.

The last of the foam dribbles from the can. I crush it beneath my heel and throw it into a box outside my trailer. It clinks hollowly against other cans in the silence.

Enough feeling sorry for myself. I turn on my heel and begin the short walk home.

You see, I don't live in my trailer anymore.

My wife, Nadine, and I have decided to make another go of it. I've moved back home. Griz has moved back home, too.

I've been away for more than a year, but the comfortable pace of home life has picked up where it left off.

Although they haven't said so, I sense my kids are happy about the reunion. Things seem back to normal.

Initially, I returned for the sake of the kids. I wanted to be near them, to help with homework, to tell them to pick up their dirty clothes, to be a part of their lives.

But deep down, I still love my wife, too, and I want to be together. Sometimes a man and woman can be so different there is no common ground. But we're searching for that common ground. Here's hoping we find it.

Now things are good. I quicken my stride home. There will be loved ones to celebrate my birthday with.

My wife, my children, my grandchild will sing Happy Birthday and I'll blow out the candles on the cake my daughter, Missy, baked.

And my life takes yet another turn.

A Hallowed Canyon That's Set In Stone

On an Indian summer kind of October day, I traipsed behind Lee Sauer into Mockingbird Canyon near Lake Mathews.

Sauer strode long-legged and loose-gaited down the short trail into a thicket of willows.

"Look out for the nettles," he cautioned. "They'll grab you."

We balanced on a log to cross a small creek. Sauer said, "Creek runs all year. One of the few around here that does."

Normally, Sauer prefers going horseback to hoofing it. He chases cattle and rides trail on a bay mustang he broke and trained several years back.

Actually, it was a horse that led him to the Luiseno pictographs we were walking to see. A former Riverside County trails commissioner, Sauer first visited the rock art in the 1980s while he was out riding with the Riverside Rancheros, an equestrian group. The Rancheros maintain a county horse trail that runs right through Mockingbird Canyon.

This trip began several months ago when Sauer, a loquacious chap, called me just to chat and during the conversation started describing the rock art in Mockingbird Canyon.

I was intrigued so I asked if he'd show me the place. He agreed and I found myself following his lead to a granite outcropping where Luisenos long ago left their mark.

Maybe it's a little ironic for a white guy to be guiding an Indian guy to an Indian site, but what the hey, I'm not proud.

First we stopped at an upright granite slab with red pictographs of rattlesnake designs on the rock. Pictographs, by the way, are rock paintings. Rock carvings are called petroglyphs. Southern California has both petroglyphs and pictographs, but Luiseno Indians who ranged from about Poway to Corona, more commonly painted rocks.

Nobody knows for sure, but many experts say the diamondback rattlesnake pattern is often found at places where Luiseno girls were initiated into womanhood.

I've got to believe it was a big deal for a Luiseno girl experiencing her first menses. Luisenos of old held a two- or three-day ceremony to commemorate the event, which included baking the girls in a sand pit with just their faces exposed. The girls were permitted no food or water and were instructed by elders in the Luiseno ways.

At the base of the painted, upright granite was flatter granite pocked with five or so grinding depressions, concave indentations where Indians ground seeds and plants with a heavy mortar.

But the depressions appeared smaller and more conical than most I've seen. Probably used more for ceremony than for food, I speculated.

Just up from the initiation site were two rock shelters, one known as the Spring Shelter, the other Winter Shelter.

To look at them, they're just a tumble of rocks. But as you get closer, you see an entrance where big granite boulders form a roof.

Sauer crawled through the entrance of Spring Shelter. I followed and sat in the sand and looked up at the paintings on the overhead rock — symbolic grids, circles, dots, a hand and chain design. The paint was red, white and some black.

In the Winter Shelter a long, net-like design in white is interspersed with red dots. Many experts associate this design with the Milky Way.

"Clearly both sites are solstice sites," said Cindi Alvitre, who wrote her UCR master's-degree thesis on Mockingbird Canyon.

Scientists have gone in and documented how the light from the sun aligns with the rock art during the solstices.

"It's a very special place," said Alvitre, who has camped here and seen the solstices.

Inside, I too felt connected to the ancients. When I crawled out, I saw big stucco houses on hillsides encroaching. Dirt-bike trails crisscrossed the canyon. Modern civilization threatened to swallow this sanctified ground.

Many of the surrounding boulders bear scars from spray paint. Taggers had squiggled indecipherable messages on surrounding rocks.

But, so far, the rock art hasn't been harmed.

"It's the power of the place that keeps it safe," Alvitre said. "But I worry."

I share her worries.

Choose Friends Wisely, Son

To my son, Bear, on his 13th birthday:

My God, you'll be 13 on Saturday, son. I'm reeling, shaking my head in disbelief, shaking my fist at the gods for allowing you to grow up.

I can still see you, a tireless tot, climbing on the couch, diapers riding low, a red bandana for a headband.

I see you in green Teenage Mutant Ninja Turtles pajamas, kicking and karate-chopping your way down the hall.

I see you staring saucer-eyed for the 100th time at "Pee Wee's Big Adventure" on video.

Yes, I have thoroughly enjoyed your childhood.

But Saturday, you'll be a card-carrying teen-ager, well on your way toward manhood. And I'll be home at nights, with holes in my socks, watching reruns of "The Andy Griffith Show," thinking that maybe some of Opie's antics may spark more memories of you as a kid.

But you're not a kid anymore. You're emerging onto the scene. As a teen, you're in for some exciting, bewildering, trying times.

For that matter, I'm bracing for some trying times as well.

But before you get too embroiled in the business of growing up, I'd like to offer a bit of fatherly advice, while you're still willing to listen.

Right now, you're my buddy. We pal around together. We go to the movies, to the beach, on hikes, on trips to Idaho. We're close as fathers and sons go.

But I expect, as your voice deepens and you start shaving whiskers from your chin, your allegiances will change and your peers will take precedence in your life.

Movies with me will probably slow down, like they did with your older brother when he decided he'd rather be with his friends. You'll want to hang with buddies you're own age. And that's OK, son. I understand. That's part of life. But let me caution you. Proceed with care. Friendships you develop now, can buoy your life or sink you.

Pick your friends with care. Select friends that enrich and add color to your life. Friends with wit, adventurousness and a sense of goodness.

I say these things son, because at your age, your vision of yourself is most likely diminished. Many teens think lowly of themselves and latch on to anyone who pays them attention.

Many false friends will drift in and out of your life. You may get a laugh hanging out with them. Or maybe they break dance real cool and are babe magnets. And they may be the bomb with other kids. But don't let their popularity rule your life.

Pick your friends not on the basis of their popularity, not on the basis of your popularity but on their quality as people.

I hope over the years I have planted seeds of quality in you. Since you were little, I have tried to instill a vision of a meaning into your life. I've tried to teach you values, tried to impart a thirst for accomplishment, tried to give you a sense of your own importance.

Hold onto these things when choosing your friends. True friends will share your vision, values and direction.

Gordon Johnson

True friends will help you become a fulfilled human being. True friends won't tempt you off the path. True friends will last a lifetime.

If you hang with lowlifes, son, you will sink to their level. As a teen you will be easy pickings for people without character, for people with only getting high on their minds, for people who want to take the easy road, such as stealing a car instead of working for it.

Remain watchful, son. Remember who you are. Be mindful of all those who love you and want the best for you. At all times carry your vision, your dreams, with you. A life without dreams is no life at all.

Oh, you will misstep. You will make mistakes. You will do things wrong. Such is the nature of life.

But if you keep your vision close to your heart, you will come out the other end of these troublesome teen years as a man of worth.

So-called friends will cloud your vision with offerings of drugs, excessive drink, fast rides in fast cars — all in the name of fun.

And I want you to have fun. But you don't need to be high to have fun. We love you. Happy Birthday!

Rekindling An Old Flame, 30 Years Later

Sometimes love dawdles. Sometimes love requires a nudge. But sometimes, even when there's no inkling of the magic at work, love happens.

For Eric Dunisch, now a 48-year-old Riverside chiropractor, and Linda Allen, now a 47-year-old social worker, the magic began nearly 30 years ago.

At the time, Linda was fresh out of high school in Washington state. Her best friend, Pat, had relatives and a boyfriend, Jeff, in Sacramento. Lured by the sirens of adventure, the girls clambered into Pat's VW van.

As it happened, Jeff had a friend named Eric. So it was only natural that Linda and Eric meet.

As youth is wont to, the foursome impulsively took off one night in Jeff's VW van, steering down coastal highways toward Disneyland's Magic Kingdom.

Now, Jeff's story was that he fell asleep and Pat's was that Jeff took his eyes off the road to steal a kiss, according to Linda. No matter, the van rolled into a roadside ditch and broke something in the front end.

Nobody was hurt, but they were stranded for three weeks in foggy Garberville, Calif. At night, they slept in a flatbed truck parked next to the service station, where mechanics worked on the van. During the day they hitchhiked, to explore the evergreen countryside.

Pat and Jeff were a couple, and they often stole off to be by themselves. That left Eric and Linda together. The two shy strangers, cast together by default, ironed out the awkwardness with conversation.

They strolled past knotty-pine cafes with signs that read "No Hippies Allowed," and talked. On misty cliffs overlooking the tossing Pacific, they talked. In an age of free love, they talked.

"I was so taken by this boy who didn't just want to paw me," Linda said. "I fell in love."

But the fairy tale ended. The van was road-worthy again. The boys returned to their rock-and-roll lives in Sacramento. The girls resumed life in Washington.

The next couple of years, Eric and Linda visited each other several times. Linda straddled the seat behind Eric on the Honda for a road trip to Eric's cabin in Truckee. Eric ventured to Washington where they boogied at a Kinks concert.

But in 1972, Eric wasn't ready for lasting love. And as long-distance love often does, the flames died and the two drifted apart.

In 1982, Eric moved to Riverside to take on a chiropractic practice. He married and fathered three children. Linda, living in Colville, Wash., also married and had three kids.

But by 1999 both Eric and Linda were long divorced. While neither had any notion of ever remarrying, sweet memories of the magic in the Northern California mist lingered.

As I said, love sometimes needs a nudge. Once again, Pat, now a Seattle psychologist, gave it one. On a recent Sacramento visit to relatives, Pat bumped into Eric, who was doing the same.

Why not e-mail Linda?, Pat suggested.

"I probably wouldn't have had the guts to phone her, but e-mail seemed easy enough," Eric said.

He tapped out a few lines of hesitant greeting and hit the send key.

"I was surprised but pleased," Linda said. "I had a million questions."

And thus it began anew. The talk. From May to August, they e-mailed thoughts, feelings and longings. Since there were no phone bills, sometimes they chatted all weekend. A contemporary kind of free love.

Over the summer Eric flew up to see Linda. They went to the drive-in movie where Eric gentled his arm around her.

"I kind of recoiled from the shock of it, but then it was nice," Linda said.

And like magic, high heels now click in Eric's living room. Eric and Linda married two months ago; a bachelor pad has become a home.

"I loved him then, and I love him now," Linda said.

Eric, full of the magic, smiles his agreement.

To A Father On His Birthday

Dear Dad:

By my calendar, tomorrow you'll be 69. Happy Birthday.

I'm sending along this CD, "A Tribute to Segovia," featuring guitarist Christopher Parkening playing Andre Segovia's Spanish music. I hope you like it. If not, you can always return it to me. It'd fit nicely into my collection.

Funny, how all these years later, I still have an affinity for Spanish guitar. I trace it to those distant days at the University Village in Santa Clara while you attended school.

Living on the G.I. Bill, we were too poor to buy a television, so the big excitement for us kids was to plug in our thrift-store record player and pick from one of our three records. There was a folksy album of American standbys that included: "Boll Weevil," "She'll Be Coming 'Round the Mountain," and "Skip to My Lou." In my mind, I can still hear songs from "Connie Francis Sings Spanish and Latin American Favorites," and finally, my favorite, an album (I don't remember the title) by Carlos Montoya, the great flamenco guitarist.

I remember taping a coin to the record arm so the needle wouldn't jump, and pressing my ear to the speaker to listen undistracted to Carlos Montoya.

Curiously, I don't give a hoot for "Boll Weevil" or "Skip to My Lou," but the Spanish guitar transports me. Images of clacking castanets, polished boot heels and swirling skirts come to mind along with a sense of my own innocence and memories of the smell of dusty carpet as I laid on the floor, listening.

And I recall the times you favored us with song. I loved the gleam of your Gibson when you opened the velvet-lined case, lifting it out like King Arthur unsheathing Excalibur.

We gathered at your feet, giggled as you tuned up, then sat dumbstruck as you strummed. Oh, out of practice, your square-tipped fingers stumbled at times on the frets, but the result was thrilling nonetheless.

A few months ago, I listened to a Mexican trio perform in a Rialto beer bar, and they played "Quizas, Quizas, Quizas," a song you played for us, and I shuddered with longing for my lost youth.

So much of you remains in me. So many of my likes and dislikes stem from you. So many of my peculiarities, idiosyncrasies, ways of looking at life are yours.

Not all, mind you. I don't guess I'll ever like creamed codfish on toast. Buttermilk still curdles my stomach. And I don't want to sing along with Mitch Miller.

But at times, I still write in a back-handed slant, in mimicry of your clear script. I guess I'll always have a soft spot for a 1957 Chevy. And if they're on the menu, I'll order buckwheat pancakes.

You know, Pops, we've never sat down and talked heart-to-heart. And we probably never will. You are of your generation, and emotion makes you uncomfortable. And I am your son, and emotional displays make me wriggle as well.

So maybe it's better that I do it in this letter. This way, we don't have to look into each other's eyes. We'll let the written word mediate between us.

But I do want you to know how much of my character I owe to you. I'm far from perfect, but I have a good side. I believe in integrity, in honesty, in working for the common good. And those values are your doing.

I'm also sorry for being so hard to raise. Now that I have a teen-age son, I realize how badly I treated you. I wasn't fair. I wasn't right. You never did anything but look out for my best interests.

But I am hardheaded, one of those who must learn from his own mistakes. And I've made plenty. And I grew up in the 1960s, when the war between the generations was at its fiercest. I am a member of my generation. I am who I am.

For too many years, more than a dozen, I guess, we didn't speak, didn't communicate. Since then, we've traveled a long, hard road together to arrive at peaceful coexistence.

But, Dad, no matter how pig-headed I seemed, I loved you. And I feel the same was true for you.

Best to you on your birthday. Your son, Gordon .

Remembering The Low Tide Of Puppy Love

Oceanside's waves unfurled flat and disheveled, not much good for surfing, so Bear and I decided to walk the beach instead of wasting about on lazy swells.

Unhurried, we made footprints along the wet sand of low tide, watching sandpipers race-walk after sand crabs, seagulls wheel and trill after a kid throwing Fritos, and winter-white beachcombers redden with their first sun.

A man in black swim trunks and a sleeveless shirt flew a kite that looked exactly like a mallard drake. Even a passing seagull was duped into belligerence.

A pale moon rose on the beach as a heavy-thighed woman in a thong swimsuit clambered up from her beach towel.

A four-pack of nymphets in shimmering swimsuits strolled the strand like it was a fashion runway. They preened and giggled and paraded.

"So Dad, what was the beach like in the '60s?" Bear asked.

Bear likes to quiz me about the 1960s. And now that he's learning to surf, he wants to hear old surfing stories too. Unfortunately, I didn't surf in the '60s. But I tell him what I can.

In the 1960s, I remember Santa Cruz and Oceanside. I told him of the longboards, the noseriding, the early wetsuits, the beach jalopies I saw.

We walked in easy conversation, the sun to our right, and I thought it a good time to broach a touchy subject. I had overheard hints that things had gone south between him and a girl he liked. Maybe it would help if I shared my own eighth-grade puppy-love experiences.

So I let Bear into my personal past: Like today, in the '60s, beach goddesses romped in the foam in two-piece bathing suits. Most beach bunnies lived to tan. They rubbed in Coppertone or baby oil and fried in the sun. They daubed on white lipstick and avoided wetting their pouffy hairdos.

But the object of my affections, Betty, was an archetypal surfer girl, who didn't fear wet hair. She had long, straight, sun-bleached locks. She wasn't tall and lanky, but shorter, with a swimmer's musculature, about 5-foot-2, eyes of blue and freckles peppering her nose.

She loved the sea. She had an older brother who surfed, so she surfed, too. Her parents owned a Santa Cruz summer beach house, and she turned coconut brown at the first sign of spring.

She had a way of standing with both hands on one hip in an orange bikini that sent me into a tailspin.

While other girls wore saddle shoes or penny loafers with their Catholic-school plaid skirts, she wore blue deck shoes — Keds.

She was the little surfer girl the Beach Boys sang about.

For a week or two, toward the end of eighth grade, mutual friends coupled up, and we were thrown together by default. It was either sit with me, or sit alone. She sat with me. After talking to her, I found we shared birthdays, a sure sign, in my mind, the heavens intended eternal love.

Lovesick, I lost weight. I stammered in her presence. Clammy jitters possessed me when I shared a chocolate soda with her.

In those days, surf boys wore baby-blue Levis, blue Keds and bleeding Madras shirts, the kind imported from India with colors that ran when washed in hot water.

Nothing else would do. "Please, Mom, please buy me a Madras shirt!" I begged. Mom bought me some wannabe Gemco shirt. It wouldn't bleed if I stabbed it with a knife. How could I wear it to the big end-of-school party? I wore an Hang-Ten T-shirt instead.

Tiki torches burned in the backyard of the big party. Betty and I danced close and sweaty to the Beach Boys and Motown. We ate steak teriyaki on a skewer with pineapple. We snuck into a darkened room for a make-out session. My, my, my. I felt skewered by her kisses.

Afterwards, I dreamed of how great our lives would be together. Ours would be an endless summer.

A couple of days later, with no hint of troubles, Betty dumped me for a friend of mine. I guess he was cooler than me. After all, he had a silver tooth.

"And so you see, son, Betty broke my heart," I said.

He smiled. And I ached a little.

He's No Fish But Finds Peace In The Water

Once or twice a week, I slip into the community pool for a lunchtime swim of 40 or so lengths.

A colleague coerced me into the pool. In years past, pools and I haven't mixed much, but he made swimming sound so rewarding, I shook off misgivings and made the plunge. And he was right. Now I look forward to it.

In the water, I wear a pair of Speedo goggles, but I'm about 50 pounds over the tonnage limit for Speedo swim trunks.

I'm an old plow horse in baggy trunks tenderfooting my way across the concrete pool apron. I lower myself into the water and push off the wall. For the first lap, I warm up with a breast stroke, frog-kicking the length of the pool, then switching to freestyle for the return leg. I freestyle the remaining 38 lengths, and finish a with five or so breast stroke laps as a warm down.

I'm a slow, ugly swimmer, relying on short, choppy strokes to propel me. When I was a kid, I admired Johnny Weismuller's powerful Tarzan strokes as he glided through jungle lagoons. I especially liked the way he poured it on when a crocodile threatened to gnaw on Jane. I've always tried to emulate his style. But I just don't have it.

I swim as a form of relaxation, as a meditation to sync mind and body.

I allow my thoughts free rein as the water beckons in blue ahead of me. I follow the lane stripe of dark blue mosaic tile beneath me. I turn my head to inhale and see blue and white flags above the pool ripple in the wind. Wavelet shadows, defined by the sun, wriggle and dance on the blue pool floor.

Choppy as my stroke is, I settle into a rhythm and stay with it. In the lane next to me, one of those sleek-bodied swimmers in Speedos blasts three laps to my one. He wears a monitor on a chest strap that counts and times his strokes per lap. I catch underwater glimpses of him as he leaves me in his wake.

In the other lane, an older gentleman wears fins and hand paddles to strengthen his swim muscles. Maybe he's two decades older than I am, but he powers through the water, also leaving me in his wake.

I fight the old, competitive urges to speed up. I tell myself, swim for the pureness of it. Don't worry about speed. Don't worry about conditioning. Don't worry. Just swim. Just turn your head to breathe. Just pull your arms through the water. Just kick your legs with muscles self-composed.

I focus on flow. On the fluidity and buoyancy of my body suspended in liquid. I set my mind adrift, lulled into meanderings.

I pass through the deep end, the 12-foot end, and I remember in my early youth my incredulity at people who swam in water over their heads.

"Doesn't matter how deep it is, son," my father told me when I was about 5. "If you can swim in shallow water, you can swim in deep water."

He failed to emphasize the "can swim" part, so in short order I climbed a diving board and jumped into the deep end. My short life passed before my eyes as lifeguards fished me out of the water.

Maybe the trauma of near drowning kept me from being totally at ease in the water. So in high school, I didn't go out for the swim team or water polo or diving.

But at this stage in my life, I luxuriate in the swim. The slow, melodic locomotion through liquid offers metaphysical solace. The turn of the head to inhale. The rumbling exhale of underwater bubbles consoles me. The sounds of swimming soothe me. The water streaming past my ears. The splash of my hand knifing through the water. The churning from the kicks. The silence of near weightlessness, of body suspended.

From our earliest moments we swim in embryonic fluids. I seem to remember high school teachers describe vestiges of gills in our embryonic development. I don't know if that's true, but we might have been water people in our primordial past. The tug of water remains strong.

In the pool, the real world disappears, and I'm immersed in liquefied apparitions. I have no bills, no deadlines, no responsibilities, just the fluid moment.

Maybe I am an ugly swimmer, but inside, I'm at peace.

Life's A Beach With Visit To Old Neighborhood

They say you can't go home again. But it's worth a try.

In a Newport Beach parking lot, where Porsches and Jaguars shone like wealthy women fresh from masseuses, my buddy, Herbie Torrens, my son, Bear, and I wriggled into wet suits.

As we suited up, young girls in candy-striped beach ware flip-flopped along the sidewalk toward the beach, deck chairs and body boards in hand. And young boys with bristly hair and sun-blocked noses winced at full-throated commands from mom: "Just where do you think you're going, mister? Stay close, ya'hear?"

I shoved quarters into a parking meter, and we joined the beachgoers.

Sunday morning, and the tourist parade had begun. Sea salt tinged the morning air. Early June gloom veiled the seascape in gray. Soft southern swells rolled in, building to jade-colored heights, crumbling to sudsy tumult.

If home is where the heart is, this is home for Herbie.

In the 1950s, brown as a coffee bean, calloused feet immune to hot sand, Herbie scrambled along this beaches like a sand rat. He lived a block away.

This is the beach where Mr. Torrens taught him to swim. This is the beach where he and his friends scurried for empty pop bottles, turning them in for deposit at Henry's, a small beach-side grocery store. This is the beach where Herbie returned his father's ashes. At this beach, Herbie still swims with Dad.

211

We entered the water. Herb, a surfer, paddled out to promising waves. Bear and I, both novices, paddled out to where the waves looked least crowded. Bear's a rookie surfer, and I'm a rookie body boarder. We prefer to stay out of the way.

The waves, about chest high, curled gently, softly, like a ringlet from a baby's forelock. And we rode without getting pounded, aloft on a watery carpet ride.

On a distant wave, I could see Herb crouched above his board, arms akimbo for balance, weight shifted to his back foot for a quick cut to stay ahead of the break.

Herbie is home, I thought.

In Herbie's day, Newport Beach was a blue-collar town, where Ford station wagons filled up at Chevron gas stations for 25 cents a gallon. Despite today's dot-com wealth, the pier remains humble, with initials and names by the thousands carved into the wooden railings.

We strolled the beach sidewalk where every crack held a childhood story.

"Along here were the fire rings," Herbie explained. In winter surf, in the days before wet suits, the best surfers gathered at the first fire ring because it was closest to the good waves. Average surfers huddled at the second fire ring, and the "gremies," the gap-toothed gremlins, were banished to the third ring, farthest from the waves.

Advancing to a higher ring was a rite of passage into an Arthurian romance of surf knighthood. Sir Herbie was a first ringer.

We walked on. There was Blackie's, the infamous beach bar, where Herbie and his buddies got tanked after a day of rugged waves.

And there was Scotty's, a fish house, where Herbie feasted on fries and fish burgers when he could scrape up the dough. When he couldn't, well, good ol' Scotty would slip him a freebie.

"Best fish burgers in the world," Herbie said.

So we sidled into a vinyl booth, surrounded by black and white photographs of Newport in the 1950s.

We ordered fish burgers all around.

Herbie pointed to an oil portrait of a white-haired gentleman on a far wall. "That's Scotty. I wonder if he's alive?" Herbie mused.

Almost on cue, an old, old man in a sweater and Bermuda shorts shuffled in.

"There he is," Herbie said.

Herbie slid out of the booth, and the two shook hands and Scotty came over to our table.

He still lives above the grill. Although he sold the grill years ago, he can't stay away. He delights in seeing faces from the past.

Some 50 years ago, Scotty developed the batter for the deep-fried fish the house specializes in. The waiter served us, and we bit into our fish burgers.

Crispy, spicy and tasty. For Herbie, it tasted of home.

He's All Aglow At The Rekindling Of Grilling Season

Press a red button on the gas grill out back and flames ignite automatically.

Click, click, click ... and poof, the uniform blue and yellow flames march along the factory burner.

Lower the lid and walk off. Come back, flip whatever I'm cooking, and leave again. A few minutes later and dinner is served.

What could be simpler? Oh, so clean and hassle free is our pricey gas grill bought from the home improvement store, but where's the challenge? Where's the guesswork? Where's the magic?

I miss the old days.

Like most boys, my earliest go at outdoor cooking consisted of opening a can of pork and beans and placing it atop a burning log in the campfire.

Now that was adventure. Even opening the can proved tricky. You had to hook the Boy Scout knife's can-opener blade just right along the rim, and leverage the blade down through the tin. Removing the lid was a most dangerous game. More than once I spiced my beans with fresh blood when sharp lid edges sliced my fingers.

And if you managed to get the can in the fire, getting it out again was a whole other story. Most campers don't think to bring pot holders. I sure didn't. I burned many a camp towel trying to retrieve a can of beans from a hot fire.

Pliers worked pretty well, but if you didn't grip the can right, the beans spilled. Nothing sadder than a good pile of beans bubbling in a bed of ash.

In later backyard camp-outs, my buddies and I made hobo stoves out of coffee cans. We punched a few holes near the bottom with a church key can opener and stuffed the cans full of torn-up milk cartons. By lighting the milk cartons, the overturned coffee can got hot enough to fry a hamburger on.

It was my first carnal experience. I loved the sight of beef sizzling on a hot surface. But ingenuity was required here as well. Holding the can while you flipped the burger had a downside. You couldn't touch the can with a bare hand or it would burn your fingers. Usually, a stick or a board placed on the backside held the can while you slid a spatula under the frontside.

More than one all-beef patty dropped in the dirt. My dogs rooted for mishaps, letting out a cheer when a burger hit the ground.

Lighting the family barbecue was something of a rite of passage, a true measure of boy becoming man.

I was so happy when I got my chance. I stacked the briquettes in a misshapen pyramid, then squirted the mound with charcoal lighter fluid. In those days, the lighter fluid had some chops. I mean it was highly combustible, not like today's sissy fluid. A few squirts and you'd better stand back to throw the match in. Too close and your eyebrows would singe.

Whoomph, the flames would jump. When they burned down some, I squirted more fluid when no one was looking. I'd heard all about fire traveling up the spray to

215

ignite the can, blowing the kid to smithereens. But, fortunately, it never happened to me.

I felt I had done a man's work when the briquettes glowed white. I swelled with pride. Eventually, my mom trusted me with turning the meat so it wouldn't burn. I was a king and my scepter was a meat fork.

When I left home to be on my own, I had to do without much, because I had no money. But one thing I refused to give up was grilled meat.

In college, I found a deep-dish truck rim and lined it with aluminum foil. I used an old refrigerator shelf for a grill. It was one of the best cookers I ever had, and it didn't cost me a cent.

A store in Santa Cruz sold horse meat. I bought some thick steaks because they were cheaper than beef and grilled them on my homemade barbecue, daubing them with melted butter, garlic and Worcestershire sauce.

Some primal instinct awakens in me when I stand before glowing coals, with a hunk of meat searing on the grill. I am hunter returned to cook my kill. I am predator sacrificing to the fire gods with prey.

I like meat. I like my meat still kicking, brown on the outside and red in the middle, blood oozing, juices flowing.

I sing the praises of the grilling season.

Now, For A Few Words From Dad

Dear Bear:

Tomorrow you graduate from eighth grade. Oh happy day! Throw the mortarboards into the air. Pen goodbyes in yearbooks. Turn up the music and dance. One phase of life concludes, another commences.

But leave it to Dad to take the pulpit at a party. I don't want to be a pissant in the sugar bowl, the "Pina Colada Song" in the midst of a Rolling Stones revue, but I do want to say a few things. Pardon my soapbox, but I'm just being Dad.

It's been a great year for me, son. I've witnessed many changes in you that I find encouraging.

You know what a nag I am about schoolwork. You know how it is with me — "Did you do your homework? Did you score well on that test? Did you make progress on that science project?" I'm on your back, because I believe education magnifies life. Sure, you can live without education, and have a decent go at it. But education colors life with intrigue, with mystery, with illumination. It adds new dimension to the commonplace. And I want a mindful life for you. I want you to live with eyes wide open.

So this year, every time you picked up a book without being told, I inwardly celebrated. It marked a big inner change in you. A newfound willingness to turn off TV and tune in literature.

And you read Steinbeck and Hemingway and S.E. Hinton and we talked about them, and I caught flashes of inquisitiveness in you. And I breathed easier. Maybe, just maybe, you will rise above the downward pull of popular culture to embrace a bliss of a different sort.

You and your peers have a hard road, son. Too much of contemporary life is driven by the buck. Too much of popular culture is a simple rip-off. And you are the targets. Take Eminem for instance. (Or better yet, don't take him.)

He's the hot, young shock rapper, spewing rage and hate like vomit. He willingly steals the innocence of youth for outrageous fortune. By conjuring the rebel image, he becomes the buzzword: "Did you hear Eminem? Isn't he radical?" Kids buy his crap so they can be radical too, to be pumped-up in the eyes of other kids. They whine and snivel and cajole to get money from parents to line the pockets of record producers and hype artists like Eminem.

But where's the artistry in his venom?

So much of the entertainment industry aims its music, its television, its movies at unsuspecting youth. It creates yearnings for high-priced fashion, for empty-calorie fast food, for unproductive hours spent numbed by video games. They clamor for your money, with no care or regard for your well-being.

Awareness is key. With awareness you can see the crassness for what it is: an attempt to reach into your pocket and take, leaving you with an empty wallet and an empty head.

With awareness you won't go willingly to the slaughter.

Now, I'm not down on all popular culture. Some of it is in good fun. But the trick is to know the difference between what adds and what detracts from life. Therein lies the secret. Awareness is the key.

Another message I hope to get across to you as you prepare for high school and for all of life — hard work, full-bore effort, pays off.

We boomer parents have failed in getting across the value of hard work to our children.

The generation that preceded us, the wartime generation, had a much stronger work ethic. In our zeal for Peace and Love, we rebelled against the work ethic. As a consequence, we haven't instilled the need for work in our kids. In many ways, we've coddled and spoiled you, given you things you didn't work for.

It was a mistake. As a result, the concept of hard work and self-discipline has suffered.

Cultivate self-discipline as an art. Be an artist of self-discipline. Say no to the candy bar or to a soda. Have a water instead. Two things will happen. You will strengthen your resolve, developing character that will serve you well for all of your life. And, secondly, when you do allow yourself a candy bar, it will taste that much better. Life will be sweeter.

Anyway, happy graduation, son. I'm proud.

Page break

Gordon Johnson

NURSERY RHYMES

I'm in the air-conditioned whisper of the hospital hallway, trying to be invisible outside my daughter's delivery room.

I fled her room the second the doctor stepped in to check her dilation. I didn't care to witness that.

Ever since I can remember, hospitals have unnerved me. I fear my presence may attract some disease searching for an unwary host. So I skulk in hospital hallways to avoid attention.

Nurses in Hawaiian-style scrubs and running shoes soft-pedal along the carpeted hallway, commenting on the tantrums of a cantankerous patient.

More nurses man a nearby station, answering phones and keyboarding medication schedules into computers. A red-faced doctor, still in his sea-foam green cap and shoe covers, scribbles on forms at the counter.

As invisible as a fat guy can be, I stand before a Claude Monet print affixed to the hallway wall. It was one of his water-lily oils, a turn of the century garden, lush and inviting. I chide myself for knowing so little about art, for being so uninitiated. But I study the scene, taking notice of the shimmering pond and the way it reflects tea-party clouds; of the bonneted woman in the long, summer dress toying with the water, stirring up ripples with a stick; of the greenery bordering the pond, the deft patches of color that describe a flowering shrub, a willowy tree, a shadowy path.

221

The pond speaks of sidelong glances over cabernet, of crinoline and croaking frogs, of poetry and stolen kisses. It was a place far, far away from a hospital hallway.

In the print's glass covering, I also see reflections of the hallway's fluorescent lights, of the perforated ceiling panels, of the mottled apparition of me.

And I think about how 23 years ago, I stood in a hallway not unlike this, and took a breather from coaching my wife through her labor pains. Funny how life unfolds. Here I am, so many years later, in the same place, suffering the labor pains of my daughter, in the same way I suffered the labor pains of her mother.

The doctor exits the room. Of basketball height, he stoops a little to clear the door frame.

"Well, looks like you'll be a grandpa soon," he says.

"Great, thanks," I say. I explain to him that my son graduates eighth grade later, so anything he can do to speed things along will be appreciated.

He laughs and says, "And I want to get home for the Laker game. We'll see if we can get baby to cooperate."

Back in her room, I look at my daughter on the bed.

Into my head pops: "Hey, diddle-diddle, said the cat with the fiddle, the cow jumped over the moon. And the little dog laughed, Ha, Ha, Ha, and the dish ran away with the spoon."

It's the first nursery rhyme my daughter learned by heart. We repeated it nearly every bedtime. Now the rhyme is in my heart, and I can hear my daughter's small voice carefully trying out the words.

White hospital sheets tent over her huge abdomen. Her lips pale. Her hands no longer childlike. Her freckles faded into dim reminders of her pig-tail youth. Only her eyes seem unchanged. Brown and flecked with hazel, her eyes still see a cow jumping over the moon and a dish running away with the 'poon.

My wife sits in the gallery of well-wishers. Her mother sits next to her. Tyra's man, Mike, Mike's mother, Mary, and Mike's sister, Tishmal, also offer encouragement.

Tyra talks into an intercom. "I don't want to bother, but I think it's time," she tells a nurse.

A nurse checks Tyra. Sure enough, it's time. She sets up the stirrups. She buzzes for the doctor. She wheels a tray of instruments bedside.

Ten minutes of pushing and panting later, at about 3:45 p.m., June 16, 2000, my second granddaughter, Nawishmal Kayleen Turner breathes her first breath.

And she's a beauty. A full head of hair, 8 pounds, 4 ounces, 21 inches long, she announces her existence with a strong, clear-throated yowl.

I exhale, wipe a tear and thank the Creator for another flower in the garden.

Up Highway One To Go Surfing Into His Past

Last week, my son Bear and I threw a week's worth of clothes, our wet suits, his guitar and his surfboard into the back of the truck and headed for the two-lane blacktop of Highway 1. We were on a road trip, a surfin' safari of sorts.

"A couple of cool cats cruisin' to Santa Cruz," I suggested.

"Alliteration?" he ventured, testing his memory of eighth-grade English.

"Exactly," I said.

We veered off Highway 101 at San Luis Obispo to catch Highway 1, and sidled up the coast highway with the Rolling Stones thrumming from the tape deck.

A patchwork of fog, damp and gray, drifted across the seascape. At times the Pacific seemed enshrouded. Other times, bright sun splashed through clearings, glimmering on the ocean chop the way a tear shimmers through a bridal veil.

Once past San Simeon, we frequented turnouts and stood at cliff edges to let it all soak in. Out a ways, the fog swirled in walls. Closer to shore, foam crashed against jutting rocks that seabirds capped with white guano. Sea otters and slick seals frolicked amid the kelp beds, dipping below the surface only to resurface again yards away. Brown pelicans dived headlong into the brine, landing with a kerplunk, then lifting off with small fish squirming in their pouched beaks.

We tooled north, over arched bridges spanning creek-carved canyons, past country stores, campgrounds and art galleries, past weathered houses perched on hillsides, houses where poets must live, penning words inspired by coastal splendor and morning coffee.

For me, the drive toward Big Sur was a drive into my past. Into teen memories of desolate beaches, where we puzzled over human folly. Why is a diamond worth big bucks, when a surf-rounded pebble, just as beautiful in its black and jade striations, commands only a snort of derision in the open market?

The raw California coast kindled those kinds of questions.

In Capitola near Santa Cruz, my buddy Craig Feeney buttoned on a fresh Hawaiian shirt, and wiped the dust off a pair of penny loafers. We had tickets for the Tommy Castro Band at Moe's Alley, a small blues club just off Highway 1.

We sipped Pacifico beers and shot the bull while Tommy set up. Like nearly everyone else, we squeezed to the front when the band fired up.

Tommy, in a black T-shirt and black leather pants, wielded a black Fender Stratocaster. A heart-and-soul tattoo emblazoned his right biceps. Tendons and sinew stretched and rippled as he ripped mercuric runs, then slowed to sweeten the notes, tenderly, caressingly, like a lover's molten look across a candlelit table.

Crowded, cheek to cheek, people danced in one spot, facing the stage. Soon the room heated up with bodies in motion, the musky air redolent with perspiration and spilt beer and cologne.

225

Tommy transitioned from funk rhythms to Memphis shuffles to traditional blues ballads. Women swoon for Tommy. Several of them could wake the dead with bluesy hip gyrations. Tommy played to them, leaning back with his Strat, rifling through electric licks that traipsed down their spines like peacock feathers at a hot-tub party.

A preppie woman in a plaid sweater vest, closed her eyes and danced side to side, her khakis clinging to her hips. A platinum blonde in platform shoes and a low-cut blouse hootchy-kootchy danced, her movements an invitation to the eyes. Other women slithered to the front just to be close to Tommy or to snap photos with pocket cameras.

Hot fun on a Saturday night.

My friend Craig lent me a longboard. Bear and I wriggled into wet suits and climbed down the bank to Pleasure Point. In the gray light of morning, the Pacific looked like slate. The ocean was glassy with indolence of summer doldrums.

Knee-high swells lazed into shore. A few surfers sat on their boards out where waves should should have been breaking, but not much happened.

Bear and I paddled until our shoulders creaked, but there wasn't enough oomph to the waves to catch them.

Or, it might have been our inexperience. But even a bad day of surfing is a good day.

Headin' Out On The Highway Not Like It Used To Be

My black pickup devours the uninterrupted miles of blacktop, gobbling up white lines.

A thousand miles to go to Coeur d'Alene, Idaho.

Inside the truck's cab, the air conditioner blows cool. A can of Red Bull, the energy drink, sloshes in the cup holder. My hawk feathers and my beaded deer antler swing from the rearview mirror. Winged bugs splat yellow against the windshield. A disembodied voice reads Sherman Alexie's "Indian Killer" through the tape deck.

I pass pickups with heavy-duty shocks pulling fifth wheels named "Gadabouts," "Happy Hours" and "My Kids Inheritance."

I follow one into a rest area. Next rest area 67 miles. Might as well deposit some used Red Bull.

An orange-vested landscape worker rakes dirt in the flower bed, careful to avoid blooming daisies. I stretch tight back muscles as I walk to the restroom.

Weary travelers recline in their tilted-back front seats taking cat naps behind mirrored sunglasses. One bearded chap brews a cup of tea in a Volkswagen pop-up camper van, aluminum teapot steaming from his propane stove. Kids rough house on the rest-area lawn, laughing and letting loose, happy to be anywhere besides the boring back seat of the family sedan, with dad mad-dogging them in the rearview mirror. A girl of about 20 in cutoff jeans and a tank top weeps into the pay phone. A break-up with her boyfriend? She's lost? Her father is leaving

227

her mother? I don't know. And I'm too socially programmed to inquire. I walk by with lowered eyes trying not to slip on her tears.

A road trip can also be an interior journey.

I drive through Utah with spotted cattle ruminating in watered pastures abutting mountains crowned by bristling evergreens.

Ranch hands in bent straw hats rip along dirt roads in four-wheel-drive Fords, a couple of Queensland heelers balanced on the wheel wells, sniffing the air for wildness.

In Utah, I buy a Double Whopper with cheese and a Diet Coke. A girl with puffy fingers and get-me-outta-here scowl hands me the food tray after calling my number. I find a seat, squeeze ketchup from packets onto the patties and eat.

I miss the blue highways of America, the slower two-lane blacktops that wind through small towns where cafes and 20-stool diners beckon.

Like the old days of Route 66, where a waitress named Dot would refill your coffee cup without being asked, and smile and chirp on about the Cary Grant picture she saw last week and how much her feet hurt.

Instead I eat alone, a poster of one of those boy bands like 'N Sync or the Backstreet Boys taped to the plate glass above my head.

In Utah, I drive as black clouds gather like an angry mob above mountain tops. Silver-veined lightning crackles through the blackness, followed by bellowing thunder. Rain drills the windshield, my wipers on high barely able to keep up.

Provo twinkles in the distance.

I pull off the freeway, and find a nonsmoking room in a Motel 6. The room is clean and white with all the personality of a hospital gown. I find a taqueria in Provo, just down the street from a KFC, and order a carne asada burrito and a tostada.

"You can't eat here," the woman says. "We're closing up."

I take my foil-wrapped food and stop in a convenience store for a couple of Rolling Rocks.

Back in the hotel room, I eat by the light of the TV, washing down the food with swigs of beer. Outside a trucker rolls in and guns his diesel engine before shutting it down. Why do that? Why gun the engine? Maybe it's like a good-night kiss, I thought.

I turn in, flipping through channels, the same channels found just about anywhere in America. I settle on the food channel and watch a chef steam a Maine lobster Cantonese style.

I look around the room. Nothing distinguishes it. Nothing gives it character. I could be anywhere in America, but I'm in Provo, Utah. I drift off as a chef prepares dessert.

In the morning, I check out, gas up the truck, buy a chocolate milk and a cellophane-wrapped cinnamon roll and hit the road again.

No Jack Kerouac here, I thought.

Taking Time For Lunch As Years Fly By

With lunch on my mind, I bellied up to the formica lunch counter at the Golden Dragon, a Chinese restaurant in Post Falls, Idaho.

A waitress with hair the color of an Irish setter's handed me a plastic-encased menu with a gap-toothed wince. Then she plunged a golden glass into a sink full of ice and topped my glass with tap water. She walked like her feet hurt.

"Would you like tea?" she asked.

"Please," I replied.

I saw a sign on the wall instructing waitresses in English, Spanish and Chinese to offer all customers a pot of tea with their meal.

Two stools over from me, a woman in a plaid Mackinaw smoked Camel Lights in between bites of sweet-and-sour shrimp.

"Oh, this shrimp is so rich," she said, licking her fingers then taking a drag.

From the menu I selected a lunch special of lemon chicken, chow mein, fried rice and egg-drop soup — $4.59.

Through the doorway and through the opening cut into the wall to allow food to be passed from the cooks to the waitresses I peered into the steamy kitchen.

A 13-inch TV burned without sound atop racks stacked with dishes. Bottles of oriental liquors stood atop a back freezer. Boxes of vegetables crowded the walkways.

A young man in a white apron, bowl-buzzed hair and wire-rimmed glasses worked a metal ladle in a big silver wok. He stir fried elegantly with veined hands that looked equally suited to violin concertos.

A young woman, the man's wife I presumed, in stone-washed jeans, a turtle-neck sweater and hair pulled back with a tortoise-shell clip, sang in Chinese as she chopped vegetables with a cleaver.

She smiled as she sang. I liked that.

I sipped oolong tea from a porcelain cup encircled by a red dragon. The same fiery dragon stared at me from the inside of my soup bowl.

Dishes mounded with steaming rice and vegetables and meats slid out to the waitresses. A bell signaled waitresses to pick up.

My waitress brought chunks of deep-fried chicken steeped in a lemony glaze, chow mein dappled with bits of broccoli, carrots and oyster-sauce beef, fried rice with slivers of pork, mushrooms and scallions.

Dragons slithered around my dish as well.

Chinese music, plucked oriental strings, rippled in the main dining room, where workmen and retired couples and young women holding babies talked of dropping temperatures, brothers out deer hunting and cussed supply houses that wouldn't deliver construction materials on time.

The busboy, a man in his 50s, with a heavy-duty comb-over that swirled over his bald pate, carried trays of dishes from the dining room to a room in back.

A vinyl apron kept his polo shirt dry. Gray flecked his reddish mustache. Bulging eyes behind thick glasses locked on to my near-empty plate.

I finished my meal and read my fortune cookie: "Friends long absent are coming back to you." I didn't know what to make of that.

I paid my bill and stepped out to storm clouds milling like soldiers before battle.

I strolled to the concrete bridge that crosses Lake Coeur d'Alene's outlet to the Spokane River. Canadian honkers flew in formation low above the water. Wind moaned in evergreens. My breath exhaled in vapors.

I felt aimless.

On the morrow, I would be surprising my parents, along with my many brothers and sisters, at a 50th wedding anniversary celebration.

I never imagined it would be like this. Walking alone on the streets of a strange northern city, hands in my pocket to keep them warm, recounting my 49 years with my parents.

My God, how fast it has all been. How the years have spiraled by.

Just yesterday I was afraid to come home after tearing the knee in yet another pair of salt-and-pepper corduroys while shooting baskets on the school playground.

Just yesterday, I drug Milkbones through the grass of our front yard to teach my Brittany spaniel to trail.

Just yesterday, I cut a heart from red construction paper and glued on paper lace for Mom's Valentine's Day card.

Just yesterday

Feral Cats, Sven's Advice, Saying Goodbye

Last week, my longtime buddy, Craig Feeney, called from Santa Cruz with news of his mother's passing.

My son Bear and I tossed clothes into gym bags, tethered a surfboard in the pickup bed and drove north to attend the funeral.

Here are some impressions of our passage.

* On a cold, star-bright night, we pulled off I-5 near Bakersfield for a burger and a chicken sandwich. We inched along the frontage road lined with gas stations and fast-food eateries, turning into a Burger King.

In the parking lot, a half-dozen feral cats sat on haunches in a circle in a parking stall. They licked at the asphalt.

"Euww, Dad, someone threw up and the cats are eating it," Bear said.

I said nothing.

We idled past the feeding cats and parked.

At night, spirits of the nether world inhabit the San Joaquin Valley. You can sense them in the purple mist clinging to street lights above Chevron stations and Taco Bells on freeway turnouts.

In the breathless night, I think of calloused hands and grumbling bellies of the Dust-Bowl era. I think of bracero grape-pickers, in straw hats and flannel shirts, clipping grape clusters from pampered vines. I think of coffeeless, frost-laden daybreaks, of aching backs numbed by force of will, of despair when there's no money to buy medicine for a sick baby.

233

From the nearby freeway, the Doppler swoosh and rumble of sedans and big-rig trucks fused with the silence the way riffling creeks and rolling ocean breakers do.

Bear and I walked toward the fluorescent-and-neon glow of Burger King, where uniformed descendants of the night spirits awaited to take our order.

* On West Cliff Drive in Santa Cruz, while Bear surfed Cowell's, I jogged the asphalt path that snakes along the sandstone-and-ice-plant cliffs abutting the Pacific. Tourists in Rockport walking shoes and matching sweatshirts, serious runners all sinew and sweat, kids in baggy pants and skater shoes, tangle-haired and tie-dyed hipsters and more, clotted the path on this sun-kissed afternoon.

In an open area, with a samba line of brown pelicans skimming along the swell behind him, sat a man in a wooden chair behind a wooden desk. Dangling from a stand atop the desk a sign read — ADVICE.

I jogged on to Natural Bridges, but on the way back curiosity compelled me to sit in the empty chair in front of the desk.

His name was Sven. He was a theater arts worker, a builder of sets and such, and a student of human nature.

The "advice" idea came to him from he knows not where, maybe from Lucy's psychiatrist stand, but he made a desk that collapses into a suitcase, painted his advice sign and set up shop.

He's been advising folks for several months now, sitting a couple of hours on weekends at different Santa Cruz locations to make himself available.

People stop and chat.

Is this a ruse, a quick-buck scheme, a way to pick up chicks? Naw, he says, just a way to talk to folks.

For the seriously mentally ill, Sven keeps referral numbers to professionals handy. But mostly it's a great way to get to know people he wouldn't know otherwise.

* Rain drummed on umbrellas at the Holy Rosary Cemetery in Colma, just south of San Francisco.

Then, like a benediction, it quit. Friends and relatives closed their umbrellas and huddled about the open grave of Virginia Feeney.

Her son, Craig, stood graveside in a new black overcoat, toiling against tears, the way Sisyphus toiled against the rolling stone.

Even the clouds seemed on the brink.

One by one, we threw carnations atop her casket. Then, to give Craig a moment alone with his mother, Bear and I wandered off to visit Joe Dimaggio's grave about 25 yards away.

Virginia, a native San Franciscan, was a Giants fan. But she forgave Joltin' Joe, also a San Franciscan, his Yankee colors.

As a gesture of their shared baseball love, Craig threw a Giants cap into her grave.

Then clenched his jaw and his fist in goodbye.

John Wayne was Hero

I blame John Wayne.

In this era of victims, when everybody points the finger of blame, I may as well too. So I blame John Wayne.

You see, I grew up in darkened theaters watching the Duke snuff Indians. I knew I was Indian. And I knew in the cinematic scheme of things John Wayne was destined to snuff me too.

But what kid wants that? What kid wants to lose every battle?

In the dark, while munching chocolate Flicks and sipping Orange pop, I shed my defeated skin and identified with John Wayne.

John Wayne could do everything. John Wayne towered above men. He walked with swagger and bravado and true grit. He spoke and pilgrims trembled. He shot ferociously, drank whiskey without making a face, roped rhinos and tossed his hat, never missing, up on the big barn's weather vane.

I wanted to excel like John Wayne. Excellence became my mind-set, my mantra. I needed to be great, not just good, but John Wayne-great at everything.

And if I couldn't be great, the heck with it, I wouldn't do it. As a result, I quit many things.

Drawing, tennis, golf and piano for example — all abandoned because I wasn't great. One by one, I let them all go, because I couldn't face up to being so-so. Mediocrity seemed the greatest failure of all.

One of my profound regrets was giving up the guitar. I loved the sound and the feel of the guitar, but I knew in my clumsy fingers that I would never be more than second-rate.

When I was kid, my father had a Gibson J-45, an acoustic folk-style guitar. Nestled in the crushed velvet of the case, the veneer gleamed with a sunburst of sound.

The infrequent times my father unsheathed his ax, I sat transfixed at his knees, feeling the sound reverberate and burst forth.

His guitar epitomized mystique. My father told of his friend, a Mexican guy who worked with him at the Fallbrook packing house. They often played guitar together and he taught my Dad "Quizas, Quizas, Quizas." Once this friend was cut in a Tijuana knife fight, and to my youthful imaginings, blood spilled with each strummed note of my father's guitar.

Later, as Bob Dylan gained famed, I too itched to play guitar. I spent hours with the Gibson, strumming from song books, learning chords to Beatle songs and the Rolling Stones and, of course, Bob Dylan. I'd wow them at parties, I figured.

For a few weeks, I even took lessons. But I judged the teacher too unhip to teach me. He had thick glasses and a bad comb-over. He wore high-water black pants with white socks and Hush Puppies. In his Wally Cox way, he had me counting notes from Mel Bay instruction books, plucking strings and tapping time to "On Top of Old Smokey," and "Camp Town Races."

Man, I wanted to rock. So I quit going to him, and forged ahead on my own, learning from books and from friends.

And I was getting decent. I had the chord changes down, and maybe even felt ready to debut. But it all crashed when this girl showed a new finger-picking style to a friend and me.

In a matter of moments, my friend had the technique wired. And he was a complete novice, starting the guitar after I did. But I choked on the finer pattern, fumbling my way through the sequence. I couldn't get it right, and the girl laughed at me.

At that moment, I knew my friend had talent, and I would forever be an also-ran.

In my gotta-be-great John Wayne way, I put away the guitar. Never played again.

It's taken me nearly 50 years, but I'm OK with mediocrity now. I got a guitar for Christmas. My daughter Tyra picked me out a Fender nylon-stringed classical guitar. A beauty.

And in my room, behind closed doors, I practice each day, a music book perched on the stand, a song in my heart.

No, I'll never be great. But I don't care. Someday, if I continue, I'll play music with my brothers and my sons. Poorly, maybe. But I'll play. And that's cool with me. It's all I'm after.

Finally, I've beaten John Wayne.

Adjusting To Process Of Growing Older

I'm a Baby Boomer. Or is it Baby Bummer?

Age spreads on me like rust on a neglected gate. I don't mind telling you there isn't much boom left in this baby.

Oh, I've read Deepak Chopra, the modern-day health guru, who contends age can be turned back, or at least slowed down, by right thinking.

He says the past is but a thought, the future an expectation. There is only NOW. And total attentiveness to the now, along with improved diet and exercise, can conquer the years, can override the body's eventual decline into atrophy.

But does his shoulder ache, like mine does, every time he goes up for a jump shot? Does his back creak and groan and pop when he bends to pick up his granddaughter from the kitchen floor? Do the calluses on his dogs bark every time he goes for a beach run?

I think not.

More and more, the conversations I have with my peers seem to focus on ailments. This, I believe, is an affliction of the aging. Even in my office, graying reporters stop by my desk to describe the latest of agonies with the bad hip or spasmy back or faulty hearing. And I listen, then contribute my own horror stories.

I don't remember ever sitting around with my high school buddies talking about bad elbows, or uncooperative knees or failing eyesight. Maybe someone might complain about an angry red zit that erupted on the chin the night of the big dance, but the conversation would end there as he gulped chocolate milk and took another bite of cinnamon roll. The talk didn't run on and on about degenerating body parts.

As I age — I'm now 49 — so many inexplicable things occur. It's not just physical decline, but attitudes and outlooks that I don't understand.

For instance, lately I find myself admiring the looks of Volvo station wagons. Before, my daydreams featured convertible Porsches zipping along coastal highways, wind in my long hair, rock 'n' roll erupting from full-throated speakers.

Now, I sometimes see myself behind the wheel of a Volvo, a nice little Charlie Byrd samba playing on the CD player. Something about the leather seats and sensible nature of the car tantalize me.

I find this frightening. Will I soon be irresistibly drawn to sweater vests and gold jump suits and Velcroed tennis shoes? Will I go into all-you-can-eat buffets and ask the girl behind the counter for prune juice with my coddled eggs?

I must confess, I've long held a fear of aging. Who in the hell wants to be old? Especially, in this youth oriented society, where oldsters seem to get overlooked, ignored like they don't really matter.

But I guess the good thing about aging is that it happens slow enough to give you a chance to grow accustomed to it. And you know what? I am getting used to the idea.

And you know what else? I'll be all right. The gray flannel pajamas are coming whether I like it or not, so why not like it?

So, here's my plan. I'm not going to worry. Sure, I'll do what I can to forestall dependency on others. I'll eat better, drink less and exercise more. And I'll go with the flow.

I've already taken up yoga, and I'm enjoying the mild-mannered approach to exercise it offers. No jarring, muscle-tearing exertions. Mostly deep, soothing stretches and careful breathing with an accent on relaxation.

And after a yoga class, I feel great — flexible and restored. And I'm all for that.

And that's another benefit of aging. I find myself willing to take things slower. I've always been a man of extremes, either a health nut, working out to excess, eating stringently, denying myself until life becomes so pleasure-less, I inevitable fall into the other extreme of the wastrel, the boozer, the cigarette hound, the fast-food junkie.

But as I slow down, and take deeper breaths, I linger longer on the things I enjoy. A good film, a stirring piece of music, a master's touch with a paint brush, a well-written novel, even, god forbid, comic books. And I find it easier to live a life of moderation.

Maybe getting older is a way of getting better.

Memories Swirl Around On Dark, Summer Night

Summer nights, I raise the bedroom blinds, open the window and place the box fan in front of the screen.

The fan, on low, sucks in air cooled by moonlight and swirls it about me as I lie on the sheets.

The fanned air eddies over and around me the way drifting water spins over and around a sun-bleached boulder or a submerged log in a summer creek.

I nestle my head into a down pillow, the one my granddaughter says smells like an old man, but the one she often chooses for her head. I've had the pillow many years, the feathers mushy with the years. But I still favor it over the characterless foam pillows also on the bed.

Night sounds distract me. Dogs barking at passing dogs. Crickets creaking like rusted leaf springs on an old pickup. Teens cruising in lowered cars, boom boxes thumping with old-school beats.

To drown the night sounds and help me switch into the sleep mode, I choose my own music.

Daylight is for listening to new, unheard music. Nights, I want songs from my past.

A small red light lets me know the CD power's on. I push play and the acoustic chords of "Suite Judy Blue Eyes," the Crosby, Stills and Nash classic, ooze from the small speakers.

In bed, I close my eyes. These songs are an anthem of my life, the soundtrack of my youth.

Some doubts arise. Was that really me in the Chevrolet convertible so many years ago, long hair tossed by unrestrained wind? Could I have been that young? That impressionable? Yes, I guess. Yes.

Into San Francisco nights we drove, toward the land of the longhairs, where freedom was the watchword, and responsibility the anathema.

And we walked the streets barefoot in leather jackets, a red bandana hanging from a belt loop of our patched jeans. And you could smell the eucalyptus leaves from the trees in nearby Golden Gate Park mingling with the cigarette smoke and the hash smoke that billowed from shadowy doorways.

And bookstores and head shops lined the streets, beckoning like caves of mystery, sitar music and sandalwood incense seeping through open doors. Women with Medusa hair roaming the aisles, braless in tie-dyed tank tops, string-tied pants and wire-rimmed glasses.

For hours, we ambled up and down the crowded streets just to let the wildness of San Francisco permeate our skin, sink into our being.

Even then, back in 1969, some cats had taken it too far. Grimy street veterans in tattered army field jackets sitting on porch stoops with a bottle of Ripple in a paper bag at their feet, staring inward with vacant eyes.

But the streets hummed with vibrancy, with the magic of change, with the synergy of deja vu. You could hear it in the hip laughter, in the quartet of congas pulsating like tribal hips on street corners, in the lawnmower sputterings of a psychedelic Volkswagen van pulling from the curb in a huff of smoke.

And you wondered what strangeness, what garden of earthly delights transpired up the flights, in second-floor flats, in black-lighted rooms decorated with Indian tapestries, Filmore concert posters and bare, blue-ticked mattresses. Where stoned, unshaven men and women, unfettered by clothes, danced the free-form preliminaries to midnight Love-Ins.

Wondrous.

In those times, there was a girl that I held sweaty hands with as we walked. She wove a sea-gull feather into her hair. And I did my damnedest to impress her with book-learned wisdom. By candlelight, she chewed the inside of her cheek in innocence as I regaled her with peyote tales from Huxley's "The Doors to Perception."

A Catholic school girl with too much trust who ventured close to the edge with the bad boy from Bellarmine College Preparatory. But we breathed in sunsets at Greyhound Rock north of Santa Cruz, where the sun dove like Apollo's chariot into the wine-dark sea, and we seemed the only two mortals on a planet of gods. Does she still see those sunsets, golden and deified, like I do?

In the dark, I listen to CSN, and drink from my life and times, as the fan whirls summer air about me.

About the Author

Gordon Johnson is a Cahuilla/Cupeno Indian from the Pala Reservation in Southern California. A newspaper man for more than twenty years, he writes columns and features for the *Press-Enterprise*, a newspaper serving Riverside and San Bernardino counties in Southern California. He studied the liberalist of Arts at the University of California at Santa Cruz, and learned journalism in the summer Program for Minority Journalists at UC, Berkeley.

He has four kids, two grandkids, a dog and lives in Pala where he got his master's degree in life, sitting under the pepper trees listening to stories from the old ones...

Printed in the United States
100471LV00006B/166/A